DYING OUT LOUD

no guilt IN LIFE, no fear IN DEATH

THE BIOGRAPHY OF A SILK ROAD NOMAD

BY SHAWN SMUCKER

Copyright © 2013 by Ann Steward
ALL RIGHTS RESERVED.

Second edition: December 2022

Published by Abide Publishers
1600 N. Boonville, Suite B&C, Springfield, MO 65803

No portion of this book may be reproduced, stored in a retrieval system, or transmitted in any form or by any means—electronic, mechanical, photocopy, recording, or any other—except for brief quotations in printed reviews, without the prior written permission of the publisher.

Cover design and interior design by Lucent Digital www.lucentdigital.co

Photos on pages 4, 68-73, 174-177, and 178 by Randy Bacon.

Photos on pages 1-3, 12, 18, 28, 36, 48, 58-67, 74, 83, 96, 106, 114, 124, 132, 142, 148, 158, 168-173, 175, 186, 192, 202, 210, 220, 228, 232, and 240 by Stan Steward. Copyright © 2013 held by Ann Steward. Used by permission. All rights reserved.

Unless otherwise specified, all Scripture is taken from the 2011 edition of the Holy Bible, New International Version®. , NIV®. Copyright © 1973, 1978, 1984, 2011 by Biblica, Inc.™ Used by permission of Zondervan. All rights reserved worldwide. www.zondervan.com. The "NIV" and "New International Version" are trademarks registered in the United States Patent and Trademark Office by Biblica, Inc.™

Scripture quotations marked (NKJV) are taken from The New King James version®. © 1982 by Thomas Nelson, Inc. Used by permission. All rights reserved.

Scripture quotations marked (NLT) are taken from the *Holy Bible,* New Living Translation. © 1996, 2004, 2007. Used by permission of Tyndale House Publishers, Inc., Wheaton, Illinois 60189. All rights reserved.

Scripture quotations marked (KJV) are taken from the King James Version, which is held in public domain.

The names of the people mentioned in Turkey have been changed to protect their identity.

ISBN: 978-1-952562-13-6 (Paperback)
978-1-952562-14-3 (E-book)

Printed in the United States of America

This book is dedicated to
Stan, Ann, Elle, and Stanley
for your courage, your love,
and your willingness
to share your story . . .

and to Maile,
for journeying with me
and always eagerly anticipating
our next adventure.

CONTENTS

PART ONE: GOD'S PRUNING

Chapter 1	*An Earnest Prayer*	5
Chapter 2	*When God First Spoke to Me*	13
Chapter 3	*I Married the Love of My Life*	19
Chapter 4	*God Began to Prepare My Heart*	29
Chapter 5	*Pruned to the Ground*	37
Chapter 6	*Struck Down but Not Defeated*	49

PART TWO: THE HARVEST FIELDS

Chapter 7	*This Thing Should Not Happen*	75
Chapter 8	*God Led Us Step by Step*	83
Chapter 9	*Our First Silk Road Expedition*	97
Chapter 10	*Kindness from the Turkish People*	107
Chapter 11	*God's Hand of Protection*	115
Chapter 12	*Traveling on the Silk Road*	125
Chapter 13	*The Sign of the Dove*	133
Chapter 14	*The Gift of God's Word*	139
Chapter 15	*Signs and Wonders*	149

PART THREE: WORKS OF SORROW

Chapter 16	*A Sixth Call to Prayer*	169
Chapter 17	*Prepared for Loss*	177
Chapter 18	*Premonitions and Signs*	183
Chapter 19	*The Doctor's Diagnosis*	193
Chapter 20	*Whatever the Cost*	201
Chapter 21	*By the Grace God Has Given*	211
Chapter 22	*What Is Your Part?*	219
Chapter 23	*Dying Out Loud*	223
Epilogue		231

DYING OUT LOUD JOURNAL   242

About the Authors   314

PART ONE

God's Pruning

Scan this code to watch a video
introduction to this section.

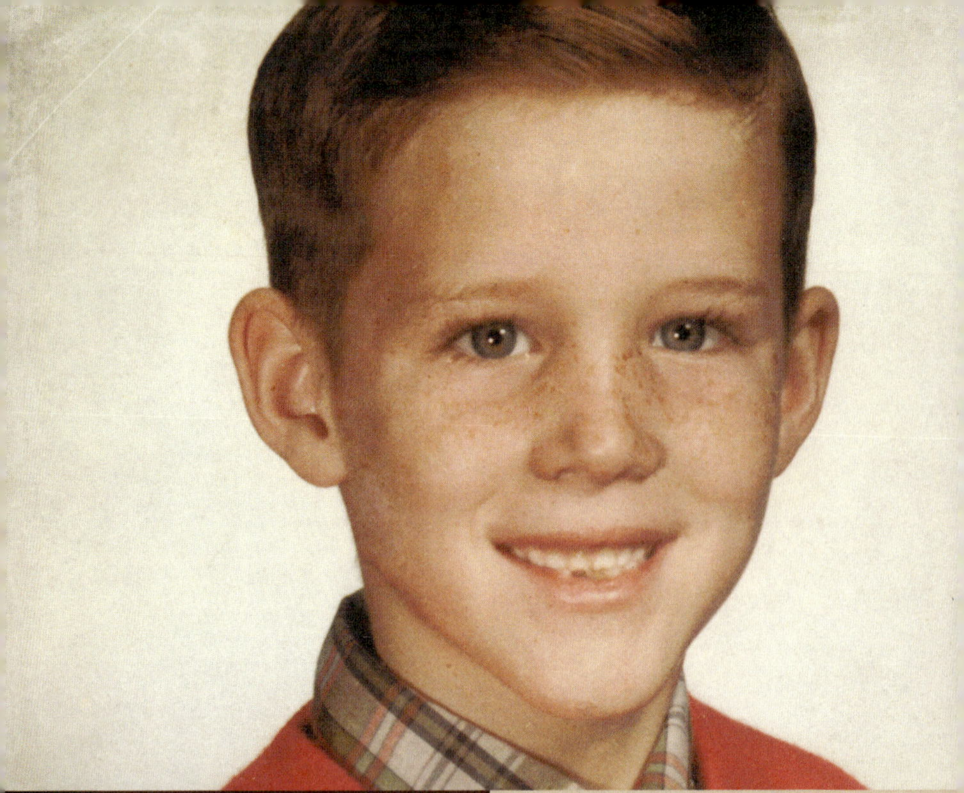

Beginnings

A photo of me at age five (top), about the time I first sensed that God had a purpose for my life; Ann at five years of age (right); and my grandparents (below). I ran to their house almost every day after school.

Finding Our Way

In 1990, I joined the San Diego Police Department—that's me in the upper left. I felt as though this was an adventure. Then there was Ann, the love of my life. These are some photos of us and the day we got married. It was one of the best days of my life!

One of the 18 million people in Istanbul who do not know Christ.

CHAPTER 1
AN EARNEST PRAYER

Though the fig tree does not bud and there are no grapes on the vines, though the olive crop fails and the fields produce no food, though there are no sheep in the pen and no cattle in the stalls, yet I will rejoice in the LORD, I will be joyful in God my Savior.
The Sovereign LORD is my strength;
he makes my feet like the feet of a deer,
he enables me to tread on the heights.

HABAKKUK 3:17–19 (STAN'S LIFE VERSE)

SOMEWHERE ON THE WINDING streets of Istanbul, deep within that 100-mile-wide city, a Muslim man closes his shop early. His name is Faruk. He shuts off the lights and turns the key that nudges the bolt into place. He steps out onto the cobblestones and walks quickly up the street.

A stiff autumn breeze moves around him. The days are shortened at this time of year, but the city remains alive and vibrant. High above him seagulls drift in the open air between the apartment buildings, wings barely moving. The birds are held aloft by an invisible force. A dove sweeps in over Faruk's head, then up under an eave, vanishing into an unseen space.

Faruk runs his hand nervously through his black hair and hurries on. When he thinks of why he is going to the mosque, his throat feels sore and tears begin, so he pushes those thoughts down and whispers assurances to himself.

In three months, six months, one year, things will be different. The doctors will see. They have made a mistake, surely. A good man does not die in this way. He is a special man—not a normal man. He will recover. Insha'Allah. *God willing.*

Faruk doesn't notice that the other shopkeepers watch him walk down the street. He pays no attention to people moving around the restaurant or the appliance store or the bank. There is the sound of children laughing a few streets over, but he doesn't hear it. A dog slinks past him and trots down an alleyway; the animal is one of many the city has tagged, given its shots and vaccinations, and left to roam freely. It growls at a pigeon pecking a piece of crusty bread. The bird flutters a few yards off and watches as the dog grabs the bread and trots down the alley, tight against the wall.

The man rushing down the street notices none of these things. His mind is somewhere else.

He turns into the courtyard outside the mosque and stops for a moment to compose himself. Why was he walking so fast? Why was he sweating? He takes a few deep breaths and then enters under the archway.

It's a small mosque situated at the corner of two busy streets. Tall apartment buildings tower above it, looking down over its shoulder. Covered with green and red tiles, it looks less like a mosque than a house from a fairy tale. Cars beep at each other on the street, and taxis dive in and out of different lanes. This is Istanbul traffic at rush hour. Chaos threatens to swallow the presence of the small mosque.

Faruk walks to the large fountain in the courtyard, takes off his shoes and socks, and moves toward one of seven stools surrounding the fountain. He holds his hands under the water and watches it run in rivulets down his fingers, wetting the hair on the back of his hands. He steps into the fountain, and feels the wet surface cold beneath his feet. He washes his hands three times without soap. It is a slow task done with devotion.

He cups his right hand and lifts water into his mouth where he swirls it around, then spits it out. He does this three times. Then he does the same thing with his nose, snorting in the water and blowing it out in a fierce spray. Another man walks up beside him without saying a word and begins his own ablutions: washing his hands, spitting water out of his mouth, blowing water out of his nose. There is a silent camaraderie there as the two men perform the ritual cleansing.

> "The future is the property of the One who plans it."
> —Paul Kocher

Faruk uses both hands to wash his face three times, starting up the top of his forehead and pulling the water down along his face, to his chin. He washes his hands and then up along his arms, letting the water drip from his elbows. He takes water into his right hand and runs it through his hair, then puts both pinkie fingers inside his ears and swirls them around while using his thumbs to wash behind his ears.

The cool autumn air spreads a chill over his wet body—the water wakening his senses. He uses the back of his hands to wash the back of his neck one time, palms facing out. The last thing he washes is his feet; using his left hand, he scrubs between his toes and up to his ankles. As he finishes, he puts his socks back on, and then his shoes.

At the decorative mosque door, Faruk is enveloped in a quiet stillness. He steps carefully over the marble threshold and onto a small stone rectangle just inside. He slips out of his shoes, never letting them touch the carpet. His breathing is relaxed now. He moves through the anteroom towards the inner room where the prayers are conducted. He has arrived just in time.

A long line of elderly men sit along the back wall on narrow, backless benches. A large chandelier hangs from the ceiling, almost low enough to touch the heads of those who walk beneath it. The carpet is a turquoise blue with dark stripes of black and gold that run horizontally across the room, perhaps four feet apart. A loudspeaker at the front of the hall proclaims the call to prayer five times a day, and there is a small alcove surrounded by decorative blue tiles where the *imam* (the Muslim spiritual leader) will soon stand and lead the people in their prayers.

"Since the first day of creation, many things have changed but *not* the will of God."
-Joseph Roth

Faruk moves in among the crowd of men and stands there quietly for a moment, eyes closed, head bowed. His arms hang at his side, relaxed and dangling. More men come in, and their arms brush quietly against the other men's arms. The atmosphere is hushed.

Faruk's socks are slightly wet and the small drops of water that fall from his hair run down his back. His arms are still damp from the ritual cleansing. He leans forward, puts his hands on his knees, and pauses in that posture before kneeling to pray.

"*Allah!*"

The imam stands at the front of the mosque and declares the Arabic word for God with great reverence, emphasizing the second syllable in a loud, distinct voice. He wears a white headdress and a ceremonial robe. He's a short man with slightly tinted eyeglasses, dark brown eyes, and a thin moustache. He has a kind smile, but there, at the front of the group, his face is sincere and earnest.

"Allah!" the imam says again, and Faruk moves to his feet.

"Allah!"

Faruk moves back to his knees, puts his forehead on the prayer rug in between his hands. Then he rises up straight on his knees, feeling the floor through the rug.

"Allah!"

He presses his hands and forehead to the floor again.

"Allah!"

Faruk stands.

He has completed one *rakat*, the series of movements from standing to kneeling to bowing to standing again. And always the imam orchestrates the movements from the front of the mosque with one word.

"Allah!"

Faruk is surrounded by other men, all praying at the mosque for different reasons. Some respond to the call for prayer out of a deep sense of superstition, a desperate need to placate an unpredictable force. Others are genuine in their quest to know Allah. They bring deep concerns for sick family members or dire financial situations. Still others want to be made pure and holy; they want the ability to think right thoughts. Some bring the pain of broken relationships, hoping for restoration. Some come to denounce terrorism and pray for peace.

Faruk begins to weep and rests his forehead between his hands on the prayer rug. This time he does not rise—he prays desperately. He begs that the healing of his Christian friend, a man named Stan Steward, might somehow be within the plan of Allah, who does not change his mind or respond to the cries of men. But still Faruk prays, earnestly hoping.

His tears soak into the carpet.

AN EARNEST PRAYER

That's me: an active and adventurous five-year-old.

CHAPTER 2
WHEN GOD FIRST SPOKE TO ME

> *We look for visions from heaven, for earthquakes and thunders of God's power ... and we never dream that all the time God is in the commonplace things and people around us.*
> —OSWALD CHAMBERS

GOD FIRST SPOKE TO ME when I was five years old. It happened the day my grandfather took me along to cut the grass at his church in Southern California, close to my house. It happened when I laid down on the small platform at the front, close to the altar. I dangled my skinny little legs over the edge and mimicked the prayer my grandfather prayed.

I was a small boy with reddish-brown hair, green eyes, and a generous portion of freckles. I grew up on the outskirts of San Diego in a town called El Cajon. It was a beautiful place. Our house, located on the corner of two intersecting streets, had a long side yard where I played kickball and football for hours with the neighbor kids. I had three sets of aunts and uncles in the neighborhood, and it seemed like there were always people beeping their horns at me or waving as they drove past the house. I experienced a great sense of belonging there, a sense of safety and security.

My dad was from Oregon. He loved trees and planted four or five in our front yard. One of them was a Liquid Amber tree that eventually grew to over fifty feet high. I used to scramble up through the branches until I could see the far-off mountains, longing to experience the world beyond my front yard. I'd perch on one of the limbs and feel the cool breeze. I had such a deep, deep desire to live an adventurous life, so much so that sometimes it made me ache inside.

"When I was a kid, I always wanted to be on an adventure. It amazes me how the desires God puts in our hearts, even at such an early age, can be an indicator of the plans He has for us."

-Stan

My mother and my father were people who prayed. I remember often walking past their bedroom and peeking in through the door to find my mother on her knees, weeping and praying to God. I remember my father's forceful prayers at the altar of our church, the way he quoted God's Word and used them in his prayers. Seeing and feeling the way they sought God with such sincerity and intensity had an enormous impact on me.

My grandparents lived a few blocks away from us and I spent a lot of time over at their house: talking their ears off, helping my grandfather, and eating their food. When I walked home from school I'd come to a T in the road: one block to the right was my grandparents' house and one block to the left was my house. I usually went to my grandparents' house. I always walked around the side of their house, unlatched the chain-link gate, slipped through the opening, then pushed open the screen door to their mudroom, and went inside. I almost never used the front door.

My grandmother's presence fills many of my happiest memories. If I happened by her house close to dinner time, she always had three places set: one for my grandfather, one for her, and one for me. I wondered how she knew I was coming over. My grandfather said grace in a serious tone, and because of his prayers (as well as those of my mother and father), I knew from a very young age that God was right there with us . . . and was listening.

Sometimes I spent the night at my grandparents' house so I could work with my grandfather early the next morning. My grandmother was part Native American, and she walked through the house quietly in her bare feet. Her padded steps made a soft sound on the hard floors. She checked on me late at night, her shadow briefly blocking the crack of light in the barely-opened door. Then, early in the morning, my grandfather would nudge me awake, and I would go with him for the day.

On the day that God first spoke to me, I had gone with my grandfather to mow the lawn at his church. He often took me to the church when he had small jobs to do there. That hot, summer day he pulled the lawn mower cord and the machine roared to life. A short, stocky man, he had white hair and stern eyes behind thick-rimmed glasses. While he pushed the mower slowly back and forth through the grass around his church, I wandered along beside him.

I loved being with him, just following him around and trying to help, and he was most accommodating. After he finished mowing the lawn, I followed him around to the side of the church and he turned on the sprinkler. The air smelled earthy and green. It was mid-day and getting warmer so we went inside.

My grandfather had built that small church with his own hands. It was the kind of place that when you walked inside, you felt like you'd finally arrived home after years of wandering. It was an L-shaped structure, a simple place with twenty-one pews arranged in three rows of seven. I guess around a hundred people could have fit in the church, but we rarely had more than fifty attend on a Sunday. Most of them were my relatives.

My grandfather started a bus ministry at one point, but it was kind of funny because most of the kids he picked up were his grandchildren. I'd sit at the end of our driveway while my parents waited in the car. The bus would pull up and I'd get on with the rest of my cousins, then we'd pull away and drive to church where my parents would pull in behind us. My grandfather had a real heart for the community, and he wanted as many people as possible to hear the gospel.

As the heavens are higher than the earth, so are my ways higher than your ways and my thoughts than your thoughts.
-Isaiah 55:9

There were four double-hung windows on each side of the church, and when he opened them a breeze rushed into that warm space. I heard the sprinkler spinning outside, and it sounded like rain on the ground. None of the lights were on, but sunrays drifted in through the windows and planted bright patches on the pews and the floor. Small specks drifted lazily through the solid shafts of light.

We went up onto the platform at the front of the church and sat close to the organ with our legs dangling down towards the altar. That's what the altar would come to represent for me: a place to wait patiently for God, a place to seek His will. Throughout my life, I've spent a lot of time praying at the altar in a variety of churches, and it's often been the place where God has spoken to me.

My grandfather and I didn't say anything while we waited there on the small platform in front of the altar on that summer day. But I felt a measure of expectation, knowing God was there with us. My grandfather leaned back slowly until he was lying down, and he put his hands together on his chest.

"Glory, glory, glory," he prayed, closing his eyes. "Glory . . . glory."

His voice sounded rich and deep. He said that one word over and over, simultaneously pleading and asking and thanking. That's how he spoke to God, and I felt a strong sense of God's presence. I knew, in the way a five-year-old boy can know, that I was in God's dwelling place. He was there with us, all around us.

I edged closer to my grandfather and then mimicked him. I laid back, put my hands on my chest, and stared up at the ceiling. I closed my eyes and waited for something incredible to happen. I don't know if there has ever been a more peaceful moment in my life, with the soft summer breeze floating in through the windows and the smell of freshly cut grass and the distant sound of the sprinkler. I imagined that was what death would feel like.

Then God spoke to me. But it took me many, many years to remember that moment, to remember what God said.

Newlyweds

CHAPTER 3

I MARRIED THE LOVE OF MY LIFE

Now unto Him who is able to do exceedingly abundantly above all that we ask or think, according to the power that works in us.

EPHESIANS 3:20 NKJV

LIFE GOES ON, and it's easy for our childhood encounters with God to fade. As children we're so open to the miraculous, but then cultural pressures set in. We're bombarded with a multitude of messages: "Color inside the lines. Stay inside the box. Think responsibly. What are you going to be when you grow up? How are you going to make a living that will support a family?" Before you know it, you have a career, a mortgage, two car payments . . . and a rigid path set in front of you.

In what now seems like no time at all, I went from being five years old to being nineteen years old. I went from being an elementary school student enamored with my grandfather to being a freelance photographer for the local paper (this meant that I only got paid for the photos they used). Deadlines and headlines and car crashes became my daily fix.

I also worked on the video team at our church. Our choir planned a trip during the Christmas holiday to sing at high profile venues in the Middle East. They asked me if I'd go along to record the choir singing and to get some footage of what those countries looked like. My dreams of being an explorer or an archaeologist lingered at the back of my mind, so I didn't need any convincing.

The day of our departure arrived. I stood in the airport leaning up against the ticket counter, day-dreaming about the trip. Excitement was mounting by the moment—I was actually going to Egypt and Israel! I had a huge passion for Egyptology. Back then, in 1981, the Treasures of King Tut were touring the United States, and even though I didn't have a lot of money at the time I bought a copy of *Baedeker's Travel Guide to Egypt*. I read it from cover to cover long before I knew I'd be traveling there. I couldn't wait to see the Museum of Cairo, the ancient city of Memphis, and the pyramids. They were places I'd dreamed about since I was a kid.

But in the middle of this reflection, at the foothills of my first great adventure, I saw her for the first time: a blond-haired girl, the prettiest girl I'd ever seen. She had almost no makeup on, and a small portion of her long hair was in a tiny braid that hung down along the side of her face. She was captivating, and images of Egypt's great wonders faded to the back of my mind.

Who is that? I wondered.

I turned to the pastor's wife standing beside me.

"I'm going to marry that girl," I said, awestruck.

She elbowed me in the ribs and brought me back to reality.

"Oh, stop it," she said, laughing.

Eventually I boarded the plane with the church group without finding out who the girl was or where she was traveling. I didn't realize she was on the same plane, traveling with the same group. It was a cold December day in Los Angeles and through my window in the plane I could see all those other planes taxiing and loading. The luggage carts swerved around the pavement. The ground crew waved in a plane right next to us and I wondered about the people on board, where they were coming from and where they were going. On that plane, I felt so alive. For so long the whole world had been rushing around me, but now I was stepping out, getting swept up in the movement.

"When I was growing up, the Apollo program was in full swing, and teachers everywhere told children they could be anything they wanted to be. But God impressed on my life that I couldn't become anything I wanted to be—I could become what He wanted me to be."

—Stan

Even though I didn't know she was on the plane, I had visions of sitting beside that beautiful girl, talking to her the entire trip. I imagined that we would fall in love and she would see that I was the one for her, that we would get married soon after returning from the trip. But she had vanished as quickly as she had appeared.

The flight to Egypt felt like a five-day journey; there were so many endless layovers and long treks through foreign airports. We finally arrived in Cairo in the middle of the night, and when they opened the doors the first thing I noticed was how all the guards walked around with automatic weapons. Their faces were without emotion, stern and foreboding. Anwar Sadat had been assassinated a few months before our trip, on October 6, 1981, so security was heightened.

The next morning I woke up, exhausted and jet-lagged, yet invigorated at the thought of spending time in Egypt. I pulled back the curtains and opened the windows and there was a beautiful little pool in the courtyard. Off in the distance I could see palm trees, and beyond them, like some kind of shimmering mirage, the pyramids. The whole thing felt tremendously exciting and new. Something stirred inside me. Something woke up.

I've always wanted to come here, I thought. And here I am. This is what I want to do for the rest of my life. Explore. Go on adventures. Wake up in new places every single morning.

But even in the midst of all the excitement, my thoughts kept circling back to the blonde girl I'd seen in the airport. Who was she? Did I dream up her existence? I got dressed in jeans and a khaki shirt, put my camera around my neck, and walked down to the breakfast room.

And there she was! I couldn't believe it! She was with our group and had been on my plane. My plane! I found out her name was Ann ... and spent the next two weeks trying to talk to her.

From then on the trip revolved around Ann. I went to the tourist sites, but in reality the entire trip passed in a foggy blur for me. I was totally infatuated with Ann and disconnected from the places we went, the sights we saw. She was a little cool towards me at first, but eventually I wore down her defenses and we started hanging out together.

In Israel I called my parents to let them know I was okay.

"Hi, Mom!"

"Hi, Stan," she said. "How is your trip?"

"I've found her, Mom."

"Found who?" she asked.

"I've found the girl I'm going to marry!"

It was a short conversation—the call was expensive—and I'm sure my mother hung up, wondering why the trip I'd anticipated for so long was no longer about the pyramids or the ancient ruins but about a blond from San Diego.

I tried to stay close to Ann during the entire trip, even though I was the official videographer. I got a lot of great footage, but no matter what amazing wonders we saw, I couldn't tear my eyes away from her. Somewhere in the world, probably in the cardboard boxes of a church's archives, there are hundreds of hours of film of Ann walking around Egypt and Israel.

The Egyptian culture captivated both of us. We imagined what it would be like to live there among the pyramids and the Muslim population, perhaps as archaeologists or explorers. We courted for the two weeks of our trip, talking and getting to know each other. We soon realized that back in San Diego we lived about five miles apart. Ann had even been to a few of our youth group meetings (where I, inexplicably, had never seen her).

The flight home was heaven on earth. I managed to get a seat beside her, and we held hands. I told her about my mom and dad, my grandparents. I told her about the little neighborhood where I grew up knowing just about everyone. She told me about her parents, how loving and supportive they were, how her family always stuck up for one another. I also learned that she had a boyfriend back in

San Diego, which was disappointing, but she said she would break up with him as soon as we got back.

"Call me when you get home?" I asked.

She said she would. And she did.

I was in love. But I was also nineteen years old, living at home, and had my parents' concerns to contend with. I told them about the amazing girl I'd met on the trip, how beautiful and kind she was. How alike we were in our desire for adventure. But there was one problem: Ann was Roman Catholic and my family was Pentecostal.

"You can't date her if she's Catholic," my dad said.

"She's a really good girl," I argued.

Inside I was thinking, *and she's so gorgeous! And wonderful!*

"Well, you can pick her up and bring her to church," Dad said. "You can even go out with her for lunch afterwards, but that's it for now. No dating."

It didn't take more than a few weeks for my parents to fall in love with her, and within six months we were engaged. Then I shuffled my feet for three years. My biggest regret in life is not marrying her the first year we met, but I was so afraid of financial insecurity. I wanted to have enough money to buy a house before we got married, so I just kept putting it off.

> "It's very easy to let your life be molded by the culture around you. But the consistent message Ann and I have received from God throughout our life together has been, If you'll let Me, there's more."
>
> —Stan

By that time I worked for the newspaper and the cable company, but even with two jobs I couldn't get ahead. Eventually I came to my senses, and in spite of my financial woes we got married June 1, 1985. There's a photo I have of the two of us walking back up the aisle, newly married. Ann's smile is slightly bashful, but you can tell she's really happy. I, on the other hand, am strutting like a peacock, shoulders back, and I'm wearing a confident grin that says, "This woman is my wife!" I just wish it would've happened in 1982 instead of 1985.

From the moment we met until now, I have loved Ann deeply. Recently we've been grieving over what has come to pass. We're willing to walk this road, and we know it's God's will, but we're also human. I've been grieving as I watch her prepare for me to die. Sometimes I can't separate the grief: how much of it is mine and stems from leaving such a wonderful wife, and how much is my grief over her sadness.

She has made this marriage everything that it is. Her ability to flow with my passions and to support me has made ours the happiest union I've ever encountered. She has met every crazy idea I've ever had with tenderness and kindness. Everything that is good about me has somehow been a reflection of her love for me.

We were traveling the day we met, flying thousands of miles on some kind of crazy adventure to the Middle East, and we're still traveling together, after all these years. It will be a difficult farewell.

* * * * * *

In those early married days, Ann worked full time as a secretary and I was still shooting freelance photography. We both had this huge desire to return to Egypt. We had fallen in love with each other there. We had fallen in love with the country. I even applied to the American University in Cairo, having no idea what I would study. We just wanted to live there. But things got busy, we became entangled in normal life, and we never went back.

We had a passion to live overseas, yet we toiled away in the US, choosing for the moment to live the life that everyone else lived—the life that everyone else expected us to live. The years passed, and even though it felt like we were getting ahead, inching forward, I had this unsettling thought that we might be pointed in the wrong direction. There was this voice inside both of us, calling us to spread our wings and make a difference for God, but with a lack of concrete steps on how to make that happen, we continued in autopilot, living the best life we knew how to live.

I had forgotten what God had said to me when I was five years old, but He hadn't forgotten. Soon, He would remind me.

I MARRIED THE LOVE OF MY LIFE

I used these situations as opportunities to pray for people.

Scan this code to watch a video introduction to this chapter.

CHAPTER 4

GOD BEGAN TO PREPARE MY HEART

Every decision, every encounter, every challenge is an opportunity for us to collaborate with God in writing our story. And when we invite God to collaborate with us, our story becomes one of redemption and love and hope.
ADAM HAMILTON

I TOOK A PHOTO of the mangled cars in the intersection. It was another sunny day in Southern California, and I was out chasing down news stories, trying to get the best shot. Suddenly I heard someone walk up behind me.

"You should apply to be a cop," the voice said. I took a few more photos of the accident scene before turning around to find a police officer standing there. Broken glass crunched under my feet. He reached out, and we shook hands. Off in the distance I could see his car parked on the shoulder, lights still flashing.

"Why would I do that?" I asked him, smiling. My freelance photography job kept me in close quarters with the officers of the San Diego Police Department, and I recognized that particular guy from a few other scenes I'd been at.

He shrugged. "Why? The excitement . . . the money."

That made us both laugh.

"I'll tell you what," he said, "would you do me a favor? Fill out an application. I get a day off for every application I turn in."

I laughed. He looked sheepish and shrugged again.

"You've got nothing to lose," he said.

"Sure," I said. "No problem."

We walked over to his car, and he handed me a few forms. I walked back to my car, then hit the streets again, looking for the next great shot.

✴ ✴ ✴ ✴ ✴ ✴

After Ann and I married, we moved 5,000 feet up into the mountains. We lived in an isolated, wood-shingle house outside of San Diego, so high up that we often got deep snow in the winter. We made the one-hour commute down into the city for many years.

But I couldn't make a living as a photographer, chasing accidents and shootings and that kind of thing. The income was too sporadic, and no matter how many photographs I took, we couldn't get ahead. Rumors circled that the company I worked for was going bankrupt. Everyone said things were going to change.

Then I got a call from the police department. They liked my application and wanted me to go down to the station for a round of testing. So I went down, figuring I had nothing to lose. One round of testing lead to another until I was accepted into the police academy.

So I became a police officer. As it turns out, I loved it. My faith started to grow as I encountered all kinds of new situations. I began praying for my co-workers, that they would see something different in me. I called out to God for opportunities to share my faith with the hopeless people I came into contact with on the streets every day. Sometimes I even prayed with people after pulling them over, instead of giving them a ticket. For the first time in my life I became acutely aware of the battle between good and evil taking place on the streets of everyday America.

> Therefore, since Christ suffered in his body, arm yourselves also with the same attitude, because whoever suffers in the body is done with sin. As a result, they do not live the rest of their earthly lives for evil human desires, but rather for the will of God.
> -1 Peter 4:1-3

What I didn't realize was that God was preparing my heart, where many of my childhood dreams were lying dormant. Sure, being a police officer filled the desire I had for action and adventure, but only just enough. God was getting ready to remind me of what He had told me when I was five years old.

Early one morning I drove home after working the graveyard shift. It had been a quiet night, and I'd managed to duck out a few hours ahead of schedule, so it was around 4 a.m. when I headed home. We'd just moved from our small cabin to a bigger place, and I stepped over boxes as I made my way into the new house.

By the time I got in and had a look around, Ann was on her way out the door, heading to work. I gave her a quick kiss good-bye. I put my hand on her stomach, and she smiled. Our first child was in there. Unbelievable.

> *"It's very easy these days for American Christians to live a good life, to serve their church and their community and do good things. But sometimes there's a big difference between living a good life and living the life God has prepared for you."*
>
> —Stan

I took a shower and moved a few things around the house. Ann and I loved our new place; it was quite a bit bigger than our old house, it had a great view, and it felt like a good place to raise our first child. After working all night, I couldn't wait to hit the hay for a few hours, but there was so much organizing to be done. Just as I was thinking about going to bed, the phone rang.

It was Ann. She had been in an accident.

She had taken my parents car, still at our house from all the moving, and on her way down the mountain she had clipped a basketball-sized rock that must have fallen into the road during the heavy rain the night before. The jolt had spun the car around, totaling it and giving Ann quite a knock. By the time I got down to the campground near the accident to pick her up, she was having spasms in her stomach. Contractions.

It's way too early for contractions. God, I prayed, *please save this baby.*

We raced to the hospital where the doctor examined her and put her on bed rest.

We arrived home, shaken but hopeful. Ann was tired and went to lie down. Then the phone rang.

"Hello?" I answered.

I sat down, covered my eyes with one of my hands, and took a deep breath.

The call was about a cop named Ron Davis. I had attended the police academy with him, and we worked adjoining precincts. He had responded to a domestic violence call at an apartment building in San Diego, and as he approached the front door, the husband of the woman who made the call jumped out of the bushes and opened fire, shooting him in the neck. He had died instantly.

I hung up the phone and stared at the table.

What are you trying to tell me, God? First Ann . . . now Ron?

I walked around the house in a daze. I sat at the table, then paced back and forth among the boxes. Life had gone from quiet and hopeful to desperate. I didn't think I'd ever be able to sleep. I looked at the clock, counting down the hours until my next shift began.

The phone rang a third time. This call was about the house we had sold prior to moving. Apparently the couple who bought the house had a massive fight and were now officially separated. They had found a loophole in the agreement, which was still in escrow for three more days, and were backing out of the sale. This meant we had two or three days to turn around and move back into the cabin we thought we'd just sold. We could no longer afford to buy that house I was standing in surrounded by boxes.

I hung up the phone and stumbled into the living room of our new house, the place I loved . . . the place we would now have to leave. I stared through the large glass windows that looked out on a beautiful mountain meadow and beyond that, a quiet, secluded road that ran beside a small lake shimmering in the afternoon light.

I fell to my knees.

God, I don't understand. What's going on? What do You want from me? I work hard for You! I'm a leader at our church, I'm on the board of Teen Challenge, and I'm a Christian cop trying to make a difference on the force. I'm trying to show Christ to the people I cross paths with on the street. I go to church faithfully on Sunday morning, Sunday night, and Wednesday night. What else is there? What else do You want?

A booming voice echoed through my mind: *"I gave you a purpose. I want* all *of you. I want* everything."

I fell on my face, my hands stretched out in front of me. Laying on your face on the carpet is hard on the nose after a while. But I didn't get up. An image came into my mind, a memory I had not revisited for many, many years.

I was five years old again. I could feel the breeze coming through the windows of my grandfather's church. I could smell the grass. I could hear the sprinkler system outside and my grandfather quietly whispering, "Glory, glory, glory." I remembered how I had closed my eyes on that warm afternoon and had felt God's presence. And I remembered the thought God had put in my mind, the first words He had ever spoken to me: *I have a purpose for your life. I have a particular task that, if you do not do, will go undone.*

Lying there on my face in a living room that was no longer ours, I remembered my response to that call as a five-year-old boy. It had felt so natural at the time . . . and so wonderful. There had been a massive sense of adventure tied to God's call. I remembered how within that place of stillness, my heart had replied: *I want that. I want to do that specific task You have for me.*

God, in His grace, used everything that happened that dreadful day to remind me of our conversation twenty-five years earlier. Peace filled me as I thought back on that day, the call of God, and my simple response. I took a deep breath, and I felt my spirit bend to His will.

It would take me forty-five years to realize that God wasn't only talking about living for Him. He wasn't just asking me if I would do all the things He asked me to do, go everywhere He asked me to go. No, He was also preparing me for something I never could have imagined. He was preparing me to accept dying for Him. He was preparing me to have the courage to allow not only my life to point others to him, but also my death.

Even if I had known that back then, I don't think it would have made any difference to my response. The strength of the calling I received at five years old was enough for me to accept God's total plan. There was a simplicity there, the simplicity of being asked a straightforward question and responding with a straightforward yes.

"Yes, God," I prayed. *"I'll give it all. Whatever You want me to do. I'll do it."*

*A father's love
is indescribable.*

CHAPTER 5
PRUNED TO THE GROUND

Christ says "Give me All. I don't want so much of your time and so much of your money and so much of your work: I want You. I have not come to torment your natural self, but to kill it. No half-measures are any good. I don't want to cut off a branch here and a branch there, I want to have the whole tree down."

C. S. LEWIS

TIME PASSED AFTER that tragic day in Southern California in 1991, and our lives moved on. Weeks. Months. We moved back into our old house. Ann gave birth to Elle, a beautiful, sweet baby girl. I enjoyed being a cop and became the link between the police department and a Christian drug and alcohol rehabilitation center in our area. I taught Sunday school and our family continued going to every service our church offered.

But all along, God reminded me of that encounter with Him. He also started resurrecting old memories in my mind. I remembered as a kid watching the missionaries talk about foreign lands at my grandfather's church. The slide show presentations they shared at the Sunday evening services captivated me. I'd grown up dreaming about taking the gospel to the far reaches of the earth.

The more I thought about that dream the more a nagging ache started to grow in my heart: there were people who didn't know Jesus Christ, who had never heard His name. How could I be comfortable with the status quo? How could I just go about normal life and have parties and get my hair cut when these people were going to hell?

Ann and I started to talk about going to the Middle East again. God resurrected that passion in our lives, and we reminisced about our trip to Egypt and Israel. We remembered how it felt to walk the streets of Cairo. We remembered how we had fallen in love with each other in that city. The more we talked about it, the stronger we felt a calling to reach those who have never heard.

> "Sometimes it's important to plan things out, to know where you are going and what roads you're going to take. At other times you just need to get into the vehicle and start driving."
>
> —Stan

About the same time, we wanted to create a way for missionaries to personally interact with the congregation, to intimately share their hearts and needs. We spoke to our pastor and asked, "What if Ann and I opened our house on Saturday night for anyone from the church who wants to come and hear missionaries speak? We'll give the missionaries a couple hours to share at our house, and then they can still have their five minutes on Sunday morning."

He thought it was a great idea. We called the meetings Cottage Fellowships, and because we were the hosts we got to meet all of the visiting missionaries. But there was one in particular who put his finger in my chest and issued a challenge that would change the course of our lives.

* * * * * *

When Abdullah (not his real name) walked through our front door, he immediately commanded my attention. First, he was a big name—an international figure—in our denomination, and his reputation preceded him. Second, he was intimidating: A short, stocky Egyptian, his heavy eyebrows and thick lips did a good job of supporting his penetrating gaze. Finally, he was extremely articulate and could speak multiple languages besides Arabic, his mother tongue.

We'd recently moved down off the mountain to the suburbs of San Diego. Elle was around three years old and Stanley had just been born. It was 1995, and life had entered a smooth time for us. But it had also plateaued, and God was getting ready to shake us again.

Abdullah stopped at our front door on his way out after one of our Cottage Fellowships and turned around to face me. He poked his index finger firmly into my chest and asked me a question.

"Are you called?"

Being a police officer, it took everything within me not to grab that finger poking my chest and break it. But something about him stopped me in my tracks. His flashing black eyes squinted, and it felt like he could see inside of me.

"Yeah," I said, suddenly feeling emotional. "We're called. We have a great passion for missions."

He didn't move his finger, so I kept talking.

"I'd love to get out from under the mortgage and the car payments. I love being a cop, but I'd rather be on the mission field."

"Who are you called to?" he asked in the voice of an inquisitor, poking me harder with each word.

"We feel called to the Jews," I said.

I'm not the kind of person to let someone keep poking me in the chest, but he just kept hitting me, both physically and verbally.

"I don't think so," he said in a firm voice. "You're called to a billion Muslims who've never once heard the gospel!"

We didn't know what to say.

What do you do with that kind of a challenge? What can you do when God is leading you one way, but the realities and chains of the world seem to have a vice grip on your life?

* * * * * *

I started studying all I could about Islam and the Muslim people. I began to feel an immense amount of compassion for their culture. You could take me to India right now, and I would weep for Indians. You could take me to Indonesia, and I would weep for the Indonesian people who are far from Christ. You could take me to Mexico, and I would weep for the Mexicans. So I can't say that we were only called to Muslims—we were called to the lost. But we went to the Muslims because it so often feels that no one is going. In Turkey right now there are 70 million people and 4,000 Protestant Christians. There is one mosque for every 3,000 people, but there are only a handful of churches.

In that moment when Abdullah challenged me, I realized that if I wanted to reach out to an unreached population, the Muslim culture was where I should be. If I wanted to live an adventurous life on the frontier, that's where it was. It was a turning point. In that moment, God flipped our calling on its head.

Then my pastor came to me with an odd request.

"Stan," he said, "we have an issue. You know that Lebanese church that's been talking about joining us? They showed up this morning, all of them. We don't know what to do other than take it as a leading of God. Will you be the point person between our church and this Lebanese community?"

"Of course," I said.

That Sunday morning, seventy-five Arabic-speaking Christians walked to the front of the church and joined our congregation. Suddenly we were extremely multicultural. We started having a joint Arabic-English service. Many of those believers came from the Middle East and from Muslim backgrounds. My interactions with them only served to fuel my passion for Muslim people.

Have you ever spoken with people who've left the Muslim community to become Christians? Their passion is unbelievable. It shamed me, how passionate they were for God. Recently an Iranian pastor came to my attention. He talked about how he gets beaten for following Christ, yet he rejoices in every situation. I realized that those Middle Eastern people were willing to go the distance, and as I got to know them better, I started to feel a thought echoing in my spirit: *There's more to life. There's a purpose that only I can fulfill. And if I don't do it, it will go undone.*

* * * * * *

Around that time, Ann planted a Black Mission fig tree in our yard. Its leaves were large and glossy on the top and the trunk split into two main sections. The branches twisted in arcs and tangled around each other. Fig trees grow rapidly.

I went outside one winter day and noticed the fig tree was over ten feet tall. The trunk was nearly eight inches thick and split into two main branches a few feet off the ground. The limbs were long and sweeping, and I knew I'd have to do something about that tree or it would take over the entire corner of the yard.

I read a book about pruning, then one Saturday I went out and pruned that Black Mission fig tree back to where it split. The entire thing fell with a crash. I looked at that pronged stump and shook my head—I hoped I hadn't killed it. I'd taken something beautiful, with green leaves and growing branches, and had lopped off all of that beauty in one fell swoop, all with an eye for the future. It didn't look good, but it was for the health of the tree, the future harvest of figs. I coated the end of it with black tar to protect it from pests and drug off the branches to be hauled away and burned.

The next night Ann and I went to church. I loved our Sunday evening services because at the end we always went up to the front with our two children, Elle and Stanley. Ann and I began every week right there at the altar. Our children grew up there. When they were babies, we placed them on the altar when we prayed, and as they grew older and could pray for themselves, they sat between our knees. Often when we walked up to the front, I remembered the altar at my grandfather's church, and how he and I had laid there, how God had spoken to me for the first time.

That Sunday night, one day after I had pruned the Black Mission fig tree, we went up to the altar to pray. We'd grown in the Lord during those two to three years since He'd reissued the call to missions. But we were still searching. We knew we wanted to serve God in a foreign land, we wanted to take the name of Jesus to people who had never heard it before, but we weren't sure how to make the transition.

God, I prayed, *work is going well. I've been promoted and we have a beautiful home. We serve as leaders in our church and in our community. But, God, I want more! I want more!*

I felt this huge yearning in my spirit that the life we lived wasn't the best God had for us. He was calling us to the next level of devotion in our lives, and I wanted to go there. Ann and I were willing to give up whatever we needed to give up in order to experience that. Then the image of the Black Mission fig tree came into my mind.

God, I want more, I prayed. *I want You to prune me just like I pruned that fig tree yesterday. Just cut the extra stuff out of my life. Cut it out and let me focus on You and the plans You have for our family.*

I pictured that fig tree, freshly pruned, cut off only a few feet above the ground. I remembered how fresh the inside of those

> *"If you are pleased with me, teach me your ways so I may know you and continue to find favor with you."*
>
> —Exodus 33:13
> (Ann's favorite verse)

branches had looked. I could see how vulnerable it had been in that moment and the way the tar spread thick over the cut-off ends.

Then God spoke to me, somewhere deep inside. *"If I prune you, I won't prune you the way you pruned that fig tree. I'll prune you like this..."*—then He gave me a picture in my mind of that fig tree cut off completely at ground level. It was totally severed, a flat disc surrounded by dirt and grass. I wondered if it could ever grow back from such a place.

But that's what God said it would take.

Okay, God, I prayed. *So be it.*

That was a challenging vision. It left me feeling both excited and anxious. What would God prune from our lives so we could accomplish that specific task He had in mind for us?

It didn't take long for the pruning to begin.

About ten days after that fig tree vision, we discovered the San Diego Police Department was going to force me into retirement due to some permanent back injuries I had suffered in the line of duty. We had no idea the doctors thought my back was that bad, but there was nothing I could do; my options were to retire or get fired. So God pruned us, and our income dropped 60 percent.

But God wasn't finished pruning us. When you ask God to cut away the extra, and He warns you that it will look like a stump cut off even with the ground, yet you still tell Him to go ahead and do it, watch out. It's painful. He didn't stop by pruning us financially; my ego still needed to be cut back.

The loss of income led to bankruptcy, one of the most humbling experiences of my life. At that time I was on the board of a Christian rehab facility as well as the board at my church, yet I couldn't pay my own bills. I was totally honest with both organizations and let them know exactly what was happening. There was just no way we could make ends meet: I delivered newspapers in the mornings along with a few other part-time jobs, but no matter what I did we couldn't avoid the stark fact that our income was severely less than our expenses.

Throughout the following year we slowly got back on our feet. We learned to trust the Lord for everything. We learned to give thanks each night for a roof over our heads, heat when it was cold, and clothes on our backs. There were times when the cupboards were totally bare and we didn't know what we would put on the table that night, but the Lord always provided. He's always faithful.

I look back now and realize that the difficulties with our finances taught us a reliance on God that has given us the strength to trust in Him throughout our lives and to watch for the miraculous when finances were needed. Sometimes if you want to see drastic change in your life, God has to do drastic things. He has to prune you all the way down to the ground.

A day came when the Lord told us to put our home up for sale. He didn't give us direction where we were to go. He simply told us, as He had told Abraham, "go . . . to the land I will show you" (Gen. 12:1). We remained painfully aware of the scripture in Ezekial 18:7 that says that a righteous man "returns what he took in pledge for a loan." Therefore we did all we could, including using the money from the sale of our home, to repay our debts.

When all was said and done, we had a little twenty-four-foot travel-trailer that we owned free and clear, along with a Dodge van to tow it, and $4,000 in cash.

So our family of four moved into that little trailer and started driving. We had no idea where God was going to take us, but we felt free and filled with anticipation. Finally, we were hot on the trail of what God had for us.

We'd told Him we wanted more, and He was answering our prayer. We drove north, we prayed, and we waited.

PRUNED TO THE GROUND

Me, Stanley, and Elle
waiting to fly to France
on our first assignment.

CHAPTER 6

STRUCK DOWN BUT NOT DEFEATED

I have chosen him, so that he will direct his children and his household after him to keep the way of the LORD by doing what is right and just.

GENESIS 18:19

ANN AND I FELT LIKE Abraham and Sarah going to a land we didn't know. We were starting over, literally from scratch. We left our families, the area where we had grown up, the church we loved, and the dear friends we'd made during the course of a lifetime. We'd learned a lot of lessons, not the least of which was to trust in the Lord. We hit the road, relying on the promise God had made to us: *I will give you more than this.*

First we drove north, followed the highway through snow-capped mountains and across vast stretches of uninhabited wilderness. We stayed at campgrounds, some hidden in the soft green of gorges lined with pine trees, others nothing more than

> "The ragamuffin who sees his life as a voyage of discovery and runs the risk of failure has a better feel for faithfulness than the timid man who hides behind the law and never finds out who he is at all."
> —Brennan Manning

small parking lots on rolling plains. We saw rivers snake through narrow canyons. We saw massive dust clouds billow across the highway. Every time we crested a peak or came around a bend, we wondered, *Is this the place where God is leading us? Is this where He is directing us?*

But we kept driving north.

Soon we entered Montana. The terrain went from rugged, rocky mountains to long, stretching plains. We crossed swollen rivers and wondered where they came from, where they were headed. We found a place that was for sale, a beautiful property that would have been perfect for a Christian rehab facility. I imagined bringing guys there who struggled with drug and alcohol addictions. I envisioned the freedom they would find there in Christ, surrounded by His beautiful creation.

We came close to signing the papers to start the process of buying that property, but towards the end I grew increasingly uneasy. Finally, I told Ann what I thought.

"I think God's telling us to wait," I said. "Let's give it three weeks. Let's drive around a little bit more and see where God leads us. I think we're supposed to dedicate more time to pray about this."

So we packed up the van and the travel trailer and headed east. And we prayed. As we drove, Ann and I found ourselves weeping, watching the passing landscape through a curtain of tears. But we weren't crying with sorrow; no, we wept with joy because we knew we were getting closer. We knew we were finally on the right road.

During this drive east, Ann had her own encounter with God. She had always imagined driving away from Southern California and living in the country, so as we passed through the idyllic countryside of Iowa, Illinois, Indiana, and Ohio, she couldn't help but hope that maybe God was taking us there. Perhaps He had led us away from the busy pace of a suburban existence so we could slow down, homeschool our kids, and live a peaceful life.

Is this where You're leading us, God? Ann asked Him during the drive east.

But then she sensed God telling her, in no uncertain terms: *If you'll allow Me, there's more.*

Whatever You want, Lord, Ann prayed.

You can settle for this, your little piece of ground, or I have more for you, came His response.

This is perhaps one of the most important messages to the church today: there is more. Regardless of where you're at right now, God wants to do more with you. He wants to use you to bring more people to Him. But it will require some pruning. He might even cut you off at ground level.

But whatever the process, He wants you to know this: there is more.

✦ ✦ ✦ ✦ ✦ ✦

In April 2001, we pulled our van and travel trailer into a small campground in Northeast Ohio called Amish Country Campsites. A narrow road wound its way through the rolling green hills, flanked by campsites and places to park campers. We backed our trailer into place, hooked up to the fresh water line, and took a deep breath.

The owners came out, a kind Mennonite couple. They welcomed us and did everything they could to make us feel at home. Over the years they've continued to be incredibly dear friends, connecting us with a network of local Amish and Mennonite churches, some of whom have become our largest supporters. The fact that we chose their campground was providential.

God had brought us a long way, from living the traditional suburban life to being nomads for Him, from living on the West coast to (almost) the East coast, from following our culture's handbook on how to live as Christians to following that still, small voice that kept saying, *if you'll allow Me, there's more.*

Yet we needed direction. We needed God to show us what to do next. So we parked our little camper there at Amish Country Campsites and dedicated ourselves to prayer.

And God answered.

The last time we'd spoken to Abdullah was at our Cottage Fellowship nearly five years earlier when he'd put his finger in my chest and said, "You're called to a billion Muslims who've never heard the gospel." But it was there in Ohio that we heard from him again.

"I'm in the south of France," he said, "and I'm working with Muslim refugees fleeing here from North Africa and the Middle East. God brought you to mind. I think you should join me."

We called our mentor, Marian Olson, and told her about Abdullah's idea . . . but it wasn't as simple as us wanting to go there. We would need to be approved as missionaries by our church denomination, and, quite frankly, we didn't fit any of their criteria. We were too old. I had never served as a senior pastor of a congregation in the United States. I wasn't even a credentialed minister and, of course, there was the bankruptcy. It seemed like a futile situation; yet our mentor graciously listened to us talk about all the ways we didn't fit the mold . . . and told us not to give up.

I called Abdullah back and explained the situation.

"We don't fit in the box, Abdullah. Ann, the kids and I would love to join you, but I'm just not sure how it's going to happen."

"Fill out the application," he said in the same voice he had spoken to me at my house five years before. "I think this is God working. Just fill out the form, and we're going to pray."

We filled out the application, and as we moved forward in the approval process all of the doors that were previously closed slowly opened. Regulations were changing, God was going before us; there were no glitches. We were approved and started our work as missionary associates with Abdullah in the south of France.

> *"Even when things seemed uncertain, we kept moving forward. I guess you'll never find out if a door is actually closed until you try to open it."*
> *-Stan*

There's a photo Ann took of us in a crowded airport terminal waiting to leave for France. Stanley is still small, wearing navy tennis shoes and a striped shirt tucked into his jeans with a brown belt. He's smiling, kicking his legs up in the air. He's always been up for an adventure. Elle leans in close to him, protective, her red bangs cut short. She's wearing a red sweater over a white turtleneck with jeans and red shoes. I'm crouching on one knee beside them, a huge grin plastered on my face. We're surrounded by a pile of pillows and carry-ons.

That was us. Just a small family hoping we could make a difference—nothing more, nothing less. Come to think of it, that's still us.

※ ※ ※ ※ ※ ※

After only six months in France, my back started acting up. I did a lot of deskwork for Abdullah, and the sitting became more and more painful. Finally, I called my doctor back in San Diego and explained my symptoms.

"That doesn't sound good," he said.

"It doesn't feel good," I joked.

"I'm afraid that one of the screws in your back may have fractured," he said. He had put several rods and screws in my back during surgery a few years prior.

> "Whatever I entrust to Him, He can take care of better than I."
> -Charles Swindoll

"So what does that mean?" I asked.

"You'll need to come back to the States for surgery," the doctor explained. "We'll have to take some x-rays and see what's gone wrong."

I tried not to get too discouraged.

"What's the recovery time?"

"In total? You're probably looking at eighteen months, once you include the consultations, surgery, and physical therapy. It's a major operation with an extended recovery time."

As missionary associates, we were only allowed one year of medical leave from our mission assignment. Any more than that and we would have to withdraw from missions.

It was with sad and heavy hearts that Ann, Stanley, Elle, and I went to the Marseille airport and flew back to the States. In fact, that was the worst day of my life up to that point. Ann pushed me along in a wheel chair through the bustling terminal, and all I could think about was how this could be the end of our missionary service. I couldn't understand it.

By the time we got back to the States, I was carrying an incredibly heavy burden. I felt like we needed to pray, really pray, and we put out the word to all of our friends and supporters, and they started interceding for me. Since my doctor's appointment was still a month away, I laid in bed and prayed. I sat in my chair and I prayed.

And God started healing my back.

After a few weeks, I could walk and the pain was almost gone. After a month, my doctor's appointment arrived and I walked into his office. He was shocked.

"What do you think you're doing?" he asked. "How are you able to walk?"

"I'm healed," I said, smiling.

He wasn't so sure. So I had some scans and x-rays done, and then we waited. When the doctor came back into the room, he looked at me with uncertainty in his eyes, as if I'd somehow rigged the scans.

"Well, I can't explain it," he said, "but I'm looking at this and it looks like the best possible doctor operated on your back. Everything is fine."

The best possible doctor. I smiled at that.

Ann spoke up.

"Would you write a letter that would release us back overseas?" she asked.

He nodded.

"Absolutely."

STRUCK DOWN BUT NOT DEFEATED

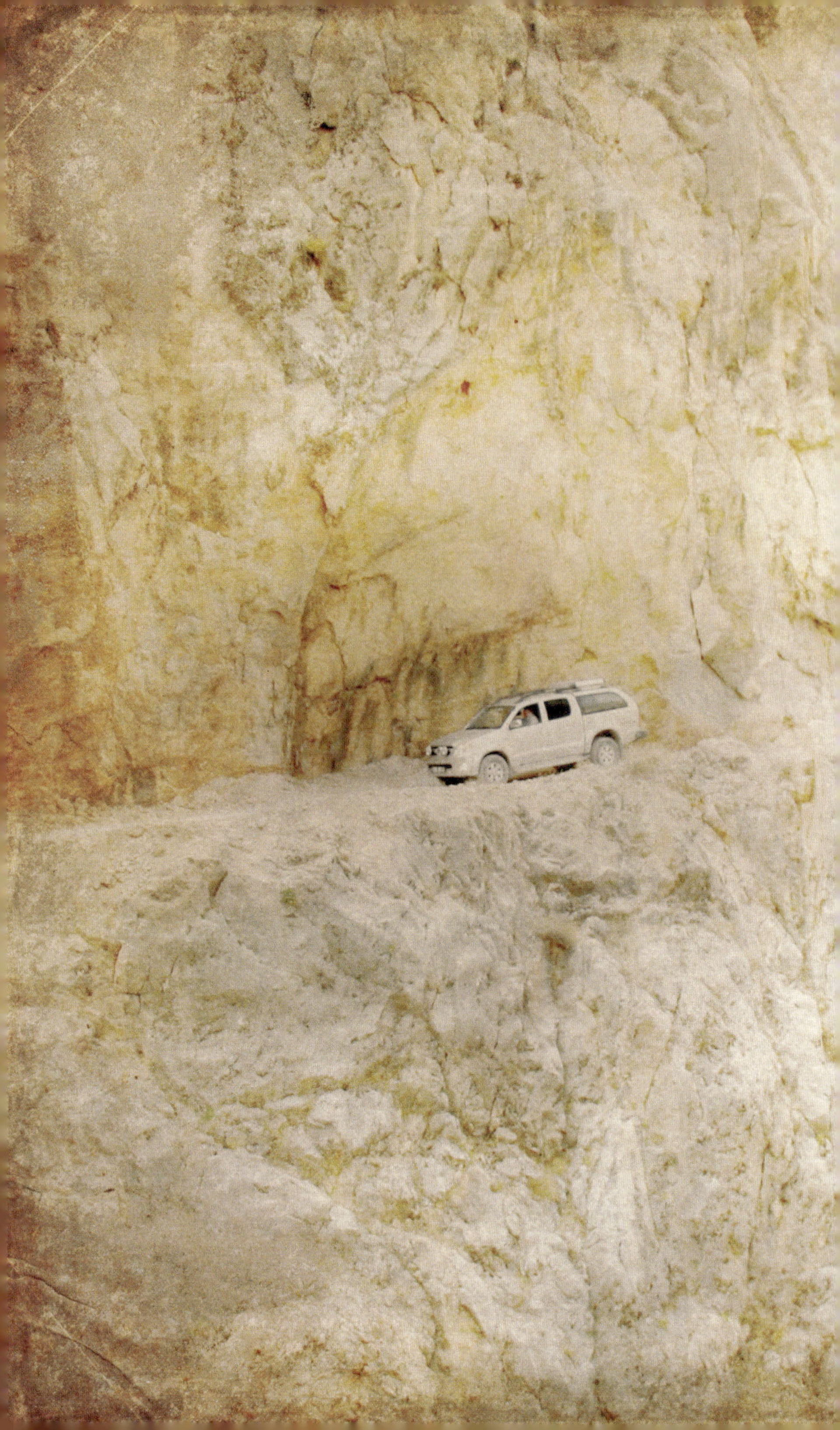

PART TWO

The Harvest Fields

Called as a Family

Whether we were traveling the plains of Ararat (top); working on the kids' schooling (middle), or trekking on the Silk Road (bottom), we did everything as a family. (Opposite) Stanley and I negotiate ticket prices; Elle crosses a footbridge of cable and wood; Stanley and I relax in San Diego in 1993.

ULUSLARARASI BİLET Gİ
INTERNATIONAL TICKET C

Silk Road Nomads

Some of our favorite times in Turkey took place as we drove through the border regions and found unexpected villages (middle). Ann spent time with the women (top), and I hung out with the men. (Opposite – clockwise from top) Ann and Elle practice their Turkish; I exchange news with villagers; Ann and a villager; marking nomadic tribes on the map.

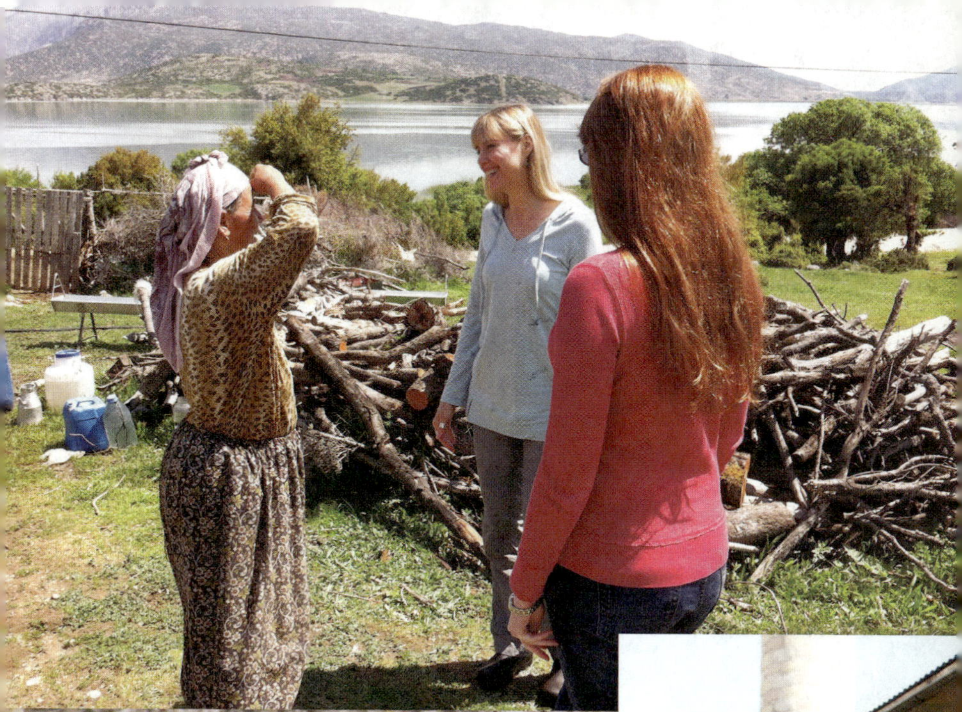
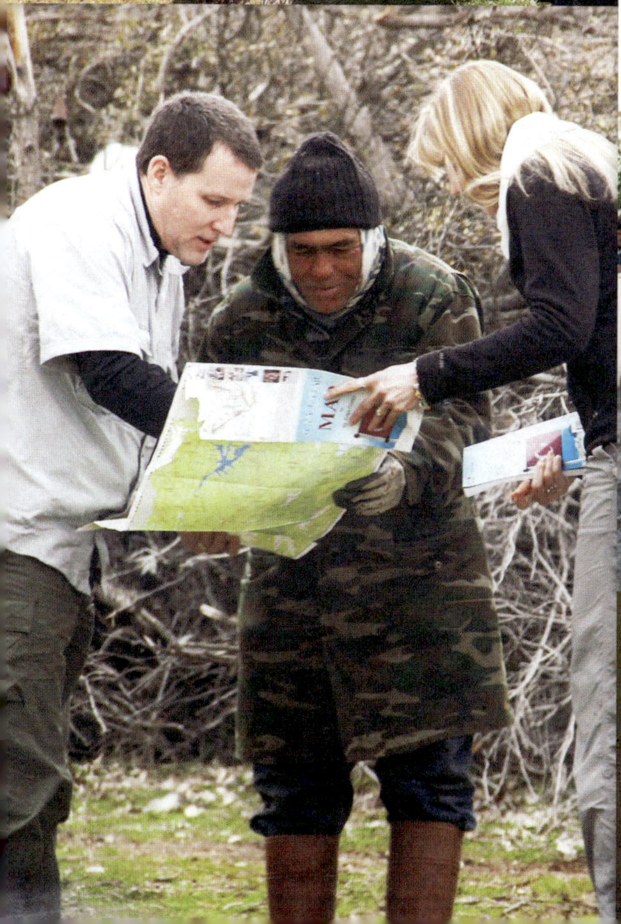
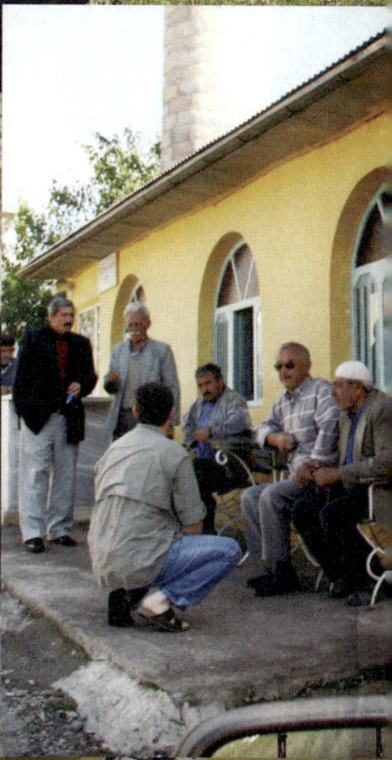
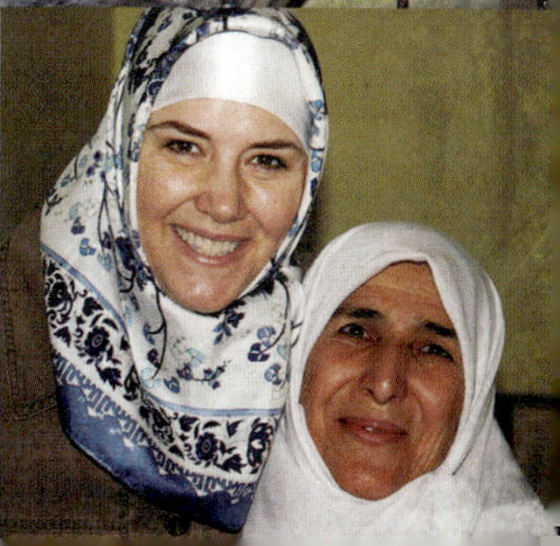

Refreshment

On our trips we were revived with refreshing spring water, (right) Turkish music, and new friends (below). (Bottom) Traveling on one of the narrow Silk Roads; making a new friend.

Travel Surprises

Whether it was looking in the side-view mirror and discovering an armored vehicle, being waylaid at a checkpoint, realizing we were headed into Iran, or making close friends in Istanbul, one thing was certain: we could never predict what would happen next!

Help at Every Turn

No matter where we went, the Turkish people were eager to help. They refused to let us pass through their villages without giving us directions, advice, and cups of tea.

Beautiful Country, Beautiful People

(Top) Planning and praying over our next journey; (left) one of the many nomad villages we stumbled onto; (middle) Ann saying hello to the children; (bottom) me and a Turkish man I befriended along the way.

Market Days

In Istanbul we shopped at the same market and became friends with the vendors. (Opposite) These Turkish men have no hope and no future unless someone shares the gospel with them.

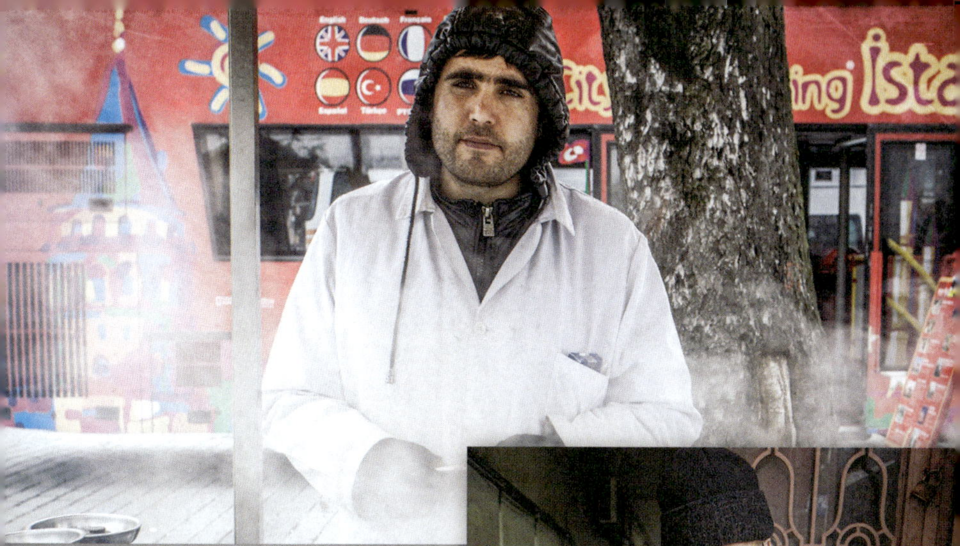

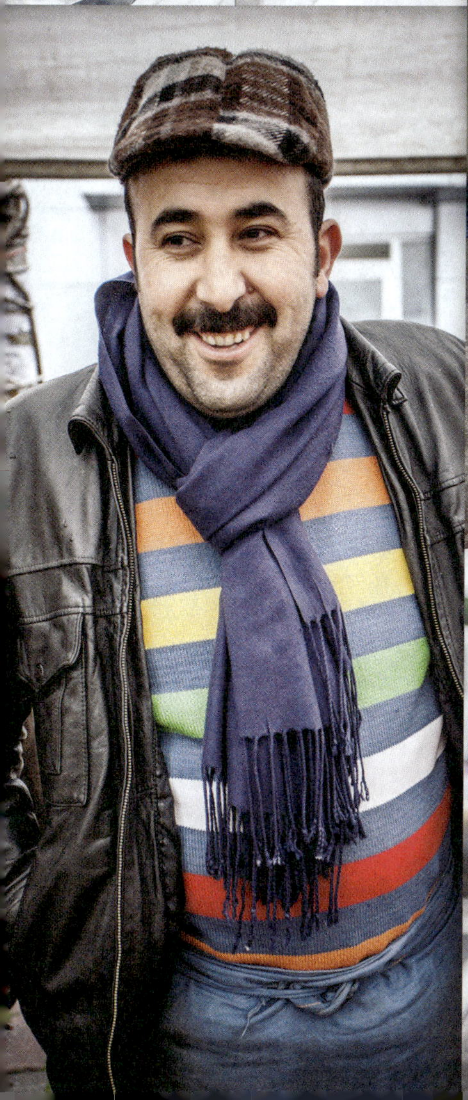

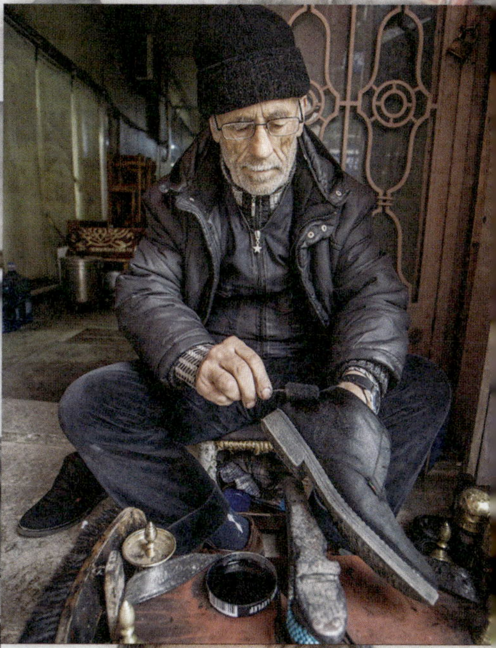

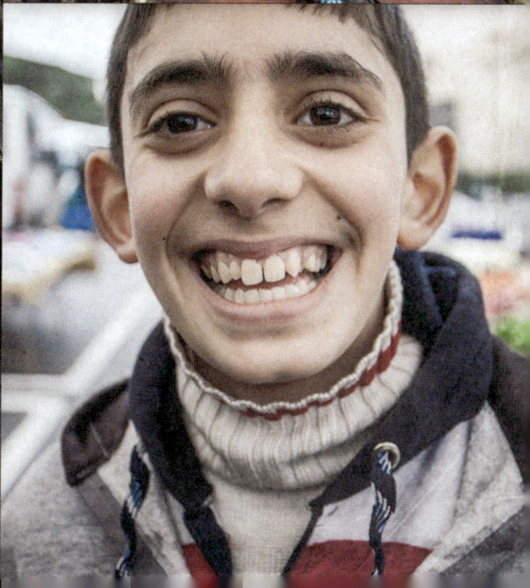

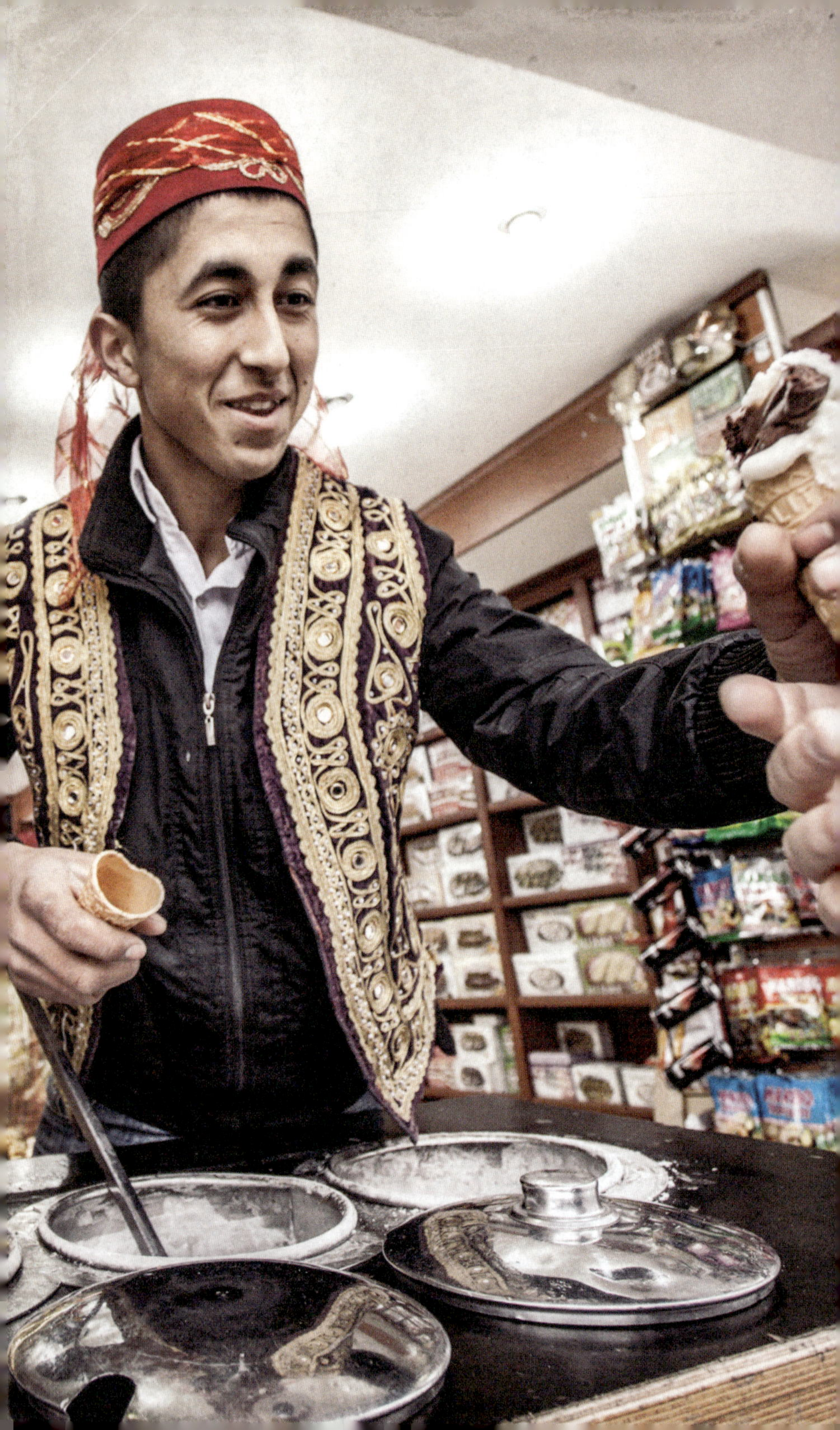

Cold Winter

Shoppers and market vendors in Istanbul—a city of 18 million people and less than 4,000 Protestant Christians.

"You Are Turkish Now"

At first our Turkish friends couldn't figure out why we would leave the United States and live with them in Turkey. Today they say, "You are Turkish now."

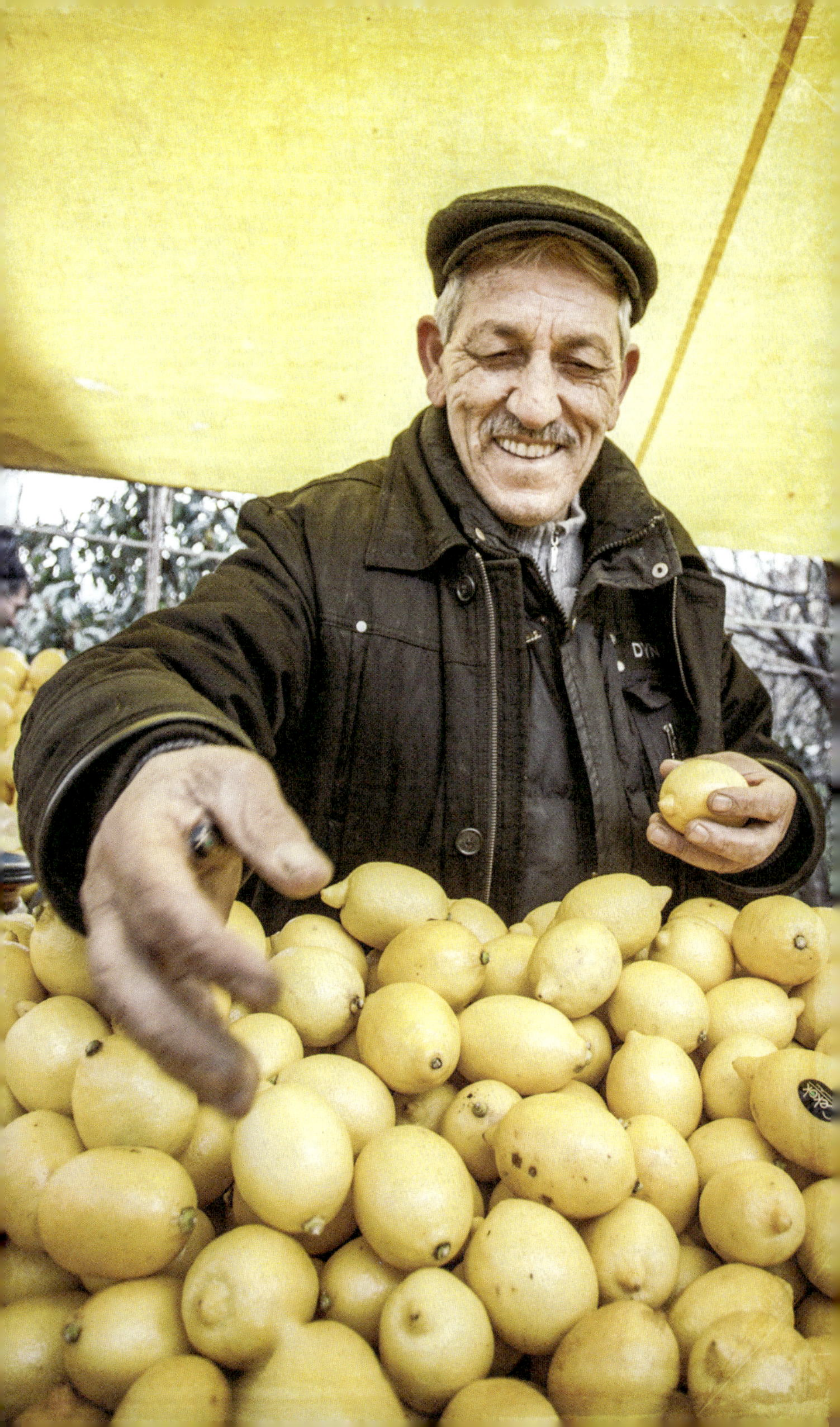

Ann brushes up on her Turkish.

CHAPTER 7

THIS THING SHOULD NOT HAPPEN

*The L*ORD *will guide you always; he will satisfy your needs in a sun-scorched land and will strengthen your frame. You will be like a well-watered garden, like a spring whose waters never fail. Your people will rebuild the ancient ruins and will raise up the age-old foundations; you will be called Repairer of Broken Walls, Restorer of Streets with Dwellings.*

ISAIAH 58:11–12

IF YOU DRIVE EAST on the winding, crowded streets of Istanbul, past the food shops and the street bazaars, past the darting taxis and the unyielding buses, beyond the two major bridges that span the Bosporous, past the minarets and the skyscrapers and the street vendors selling sesame-coated *simit* bread, you'll notice the city begin to thin out. Apartment buildings give way to townhouses and single-family dwellings. Eventually, you'll leave the city behind, hidden by the rolling hills on which it's built.

> *"However rough and difficult the path, ever remember that you are being led by Him who has mercy on you."*
>
> —F. B. Meyer

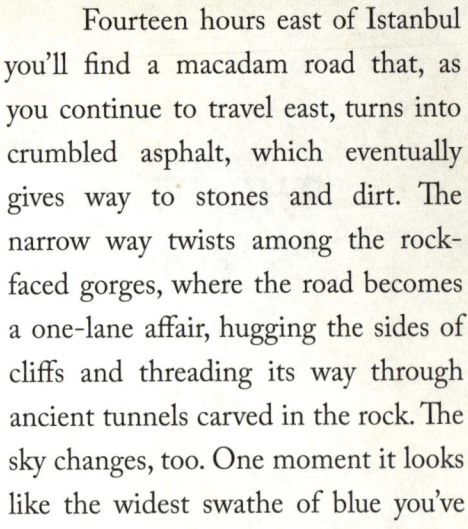

Fourteen hours east of Istanbul you'll find a macadam road that, as you continue to travel east, turns into crumbled asphalt, which eventually gives way to stones and dirt. The narrow way twists among the rock-faced gorges, where the road becomes a one-lane affair, hugging the sides of cliffs and threading its way through ancient tunnels carved in the rock. The sky changes, too. One moment it looks like the widest swathe of blue you've ever seen; the next moment all you can see is a narrow strip of blue visible from the floor of a deep canyon.

One of the most dominant features of eastern Turkey is the Euphrates River. It's an ancient river that has worn through the stone and the earth for thousands of years and still flows steadily south towards Syria. Not too much farther east is the Tigris River, which also flows south into Iraq. For hundreds of years the ancient silk roads passed through this region and allowed trade between China, India, Persia, Europe, and Arabia.

Hidden in the depths of this wild area, and lining the Euphrates, is the Dark Canyon, made up of gorges and hillsides, grasslands and rock formations etched and sustained by the river. And while the roads in the Dark Canyon are no longer used to trade silk and spices or to build empires, they are still frequented by nomadic herdsmen. As you drive these ancient roads, you pass village after village—thousands of small communities representing hundreds of thousands of people.

Perhaps a handful of them have ever heard the gospel.

Yet a deep vein of Christianity is buried there, not far beneath the surface. Wandering through the mountain paths, you might happen upon the remains of old churches, abandoned and empty; these structures have succumbed to nature. Roofs have crumbled; foundations have cracked. Large trees grow up through the gaping holes. Birds nest in the eaves.

But this decay has not been facilitated by nature alone. Throughout the years, locals have come and removed or erased the images of the cross. This is a political and historical move as much as a religious one: the Christian cross is a symbol of the West that hearkens back to the Crusades. It's an image that many see to be in direct contradiction with Turkish heritage.

So a country that at one time served as the central seat of Christianity, the country that once was home to the city of Constantinople, the country that once welcomed Paul on many of his journeys, is now the dwelling place of Islam. The churches that avoided being turned into museums or falling victim to the dereliction of time have been turned into mosques with minarets added and interiors redesigned so that attendants can face Mecca when they pray. The reminders of a Christian heritage have been spackled over, but if you look closely you can still see the faded shadows on the stones where crosses used to be.

* * * * * *

In one of these Dark Canyon villages, a woman named Emine works inside her home. She's short and always covers her hair with decorative scarves, some with dangling beads that frame her face.

Her large brown eyes squint when she smiles. She usually dresses in blue-green or violet.

Her house is perched on the steep cliffs that lead down to the green, steady current of the Euphrates. The land surrounding the village alternates between bare rock and short scruffy shrubs. The streets are rutted and muddy, pooling with water after the rain. Some of the people who live there are nomadic; they toil hard to make a living off the land. They spend the summers in the mountains where there is water and sun-scorched pastures for their livestock. In the winter they leave the snow behind and settle in the warmer valleys. Season after season they shuttle back and forth, generation after generation.

Emine sweeps and cooks and waits for her son to come home from school. Her house is impeccably clean and smells of fresh bread. Large rugs cover the floors, and the walls are a shade of cream. It's not a big house, but is sufficient for her, her husband, and their son.

> "The purpose of life is a life of purpose."
> —Robert Byrne

The water pot boils, and she removes it from the heat. Suddenly, the telephone rings. She leans the stiff broom against the wall and glances at her work before answering. It's her friend from Istanbul, Ann. She's a Christian woman—a bright light of kindness in what often feels like a drab, hopeless life. They spend a few minutes talking about everyday things: her own husband's work, her son, the weather in the Dark Canyon.

Ann is helping Emine build a small business by selling her handmade scarves in Istanbul. Ann tells how many new scarves she needs and how many she has sold. Emine smiles and whispers thanks to Allah for money to pay her bills. She dreams of the day she can sell enough scarves to give her son a better life.

Emine remembers how, just a few weeks before, Ann and her husband, Stan, and their son, Stanley, had visited their village. Ann and Stan offered to pray with Emine, her husband, her sister, and her brother-in-law. The seven of them prayed together right there on the street in their village. Stan prayed specifically that Emine's husband would find work, and then he prayed in a different language, one she was not familiar with.

The group opened their eyes after the prayer, and Emine's sister was beaming.

"I understood that inside!" she said, referring to Stan's prayer in the strange language.

Now Ann is saying something on the telephone that makes Emine feel around for a chair. She sits down.

"No . . . no . . . no," Emine mumbles.

Ann's voice continues on the other end of the line, trying to bring comfort.

"No . . . no . . . no," Emine says again, her voice beginning to rise. She refuses to believe what Ann has just told her.

Ann's voice comes faster now on the phone, trying to head off the approaching grief.

"I can't believe it," Emine says between the sobs that grow stronger and stronger. "You have such clean hearts. Allah answers your prayers. This cannot be."

Soon her comments turn into one long, wailing sob. Her shoulders shake and she finds it hard to breathe. Tears blind her. Now Ann's voice comes slowly and steadily on the other end of the line, trying to get the woman's attention, trying to alleviate her heartache. Ann tries to convince Ermine to take the phone to the neighbor, but Emine will not get up.

Emine remembers when Ann and her family first came to their village. They'd been a curiosity, that American family driving a 4X4, bringing along their young children. But they'd respected the villagers and their traditions. They'd taken off their shoes in the house, they'd eaten what was given to them, and they'd tried to learn new words . . . the words of the villagers.

As Emine sits to recollect her thoughts, her family comes running into her home.

"What's wrong?"

"Who is it?"

"What's happening?"

Meanwhile, Ann is still speaking calmly on the other end of the line, reassuring Emine, "It's going to be okay. We're at peace; we're in God's hands." Ann can only pray with Emine and call on God to comfort her.

But Emine cannot listen to the voice on the phone. Her own grief is much too loud.

Emine hangs up, then calls her husband who is working at his new job in construction. He immediately pulls off of the road and goes into the closest mosque to pray to Allah on behalf of Stan.

Later that day, the neighbors gather around, and when Emine is finally able to give them the news about Stan, the women begin to weep and the men pace back and forth. Word passes quickly through the valleys and villages of the Dark Canyon.

That night, and for many nights to come, Muslim people throughout the Dark Canyon will fill their mosques with prayers for their Christian friends, Stan and Ann Steward. They cannot understand how Allah would allow such a thing. So the men prostrate themselves, their foreheads pressing the carpet, their tears soaking into its fabric. The women, too, say their prayers and hope that it's Allah's will that this thing should not happen.

*Elle and Stanley,
ages six and three.*

CHAPTER 8
GOD LED US STEP BY STEP

I am ready to go anywhere, provided it be forward.
DAVID LIVINGSTONE

SOON AFTER GOD healed my back, we began the process of seeking where He wanted us to go as career missionaries. We met with our denomination's Director over Europe and Asia. We talked to him about our desire to go where no one was working. I will never forget his words.

"If I gave you a white board that you could write anything on, what would you write?"

Even though we knew no one was able to get into the country, I said, "Iran."

He picked up the phone and called Marc Luther.

Marc was extremely knowledgeable about the Muslim world and Islamic countries in general so we planned a trip to Cyprus to meet with him. The tickets were expensive, and it was a long flight for what would be a rather short stay, so Ann and I decided to go without the kids. We'd never traveled without them up until that point, but we just didn't have the money for four tickets.

The kids were going to stay with my parents, but everyone came along to the airport to drop us off. We stood there, waiting to check in, when Elle and Stanley looked up at Ann and I. They were disappointed that we would go on a trip without them. Then Elle, twelve years old at the time, said something that has stayed in my mind ever since.

"We were called to the mission field together, as a family," she said with tears in her eyes. "We're stronger together. And you're going without us?"

Stanley stood there beside her, and there was a lot of hurt and confusion on his face. Elle was right, of course. We'd done everything up to that point as a family. We'd prayed together every night, talked about where God might be leading us, and often listened to the discernment of our children when making decisions. I boarded that plane and resolved never to leave the kids behind again.

After that, we told our director that we wouldn't travel anywhere unless we could go as a family. We believed that making decisions together, as a family, would draw our children closer to the Lord and help them grow in their love for missions. We did our best to recognize the familial nature of our calling. Some in ministry and missions have sacrificed their children on the altar of ministry, but I've always believed that God's priority for me is to take care of my wife and my kids first and do ministry after that. We're so grateful for leadership that has supported our family's call and our decision not to travel without our children.

It's one of the best decisions we've made.

✶ ✶ ✶ ✶ ✶ ✶

In November, 2004, Ann and I arrived in Cyprus. We were eager to seek out any information Marc might have about getting into Iran. We so desperately wanted to get back to the mission field, to start sharing Christ with people who'd never heard the gospel. It wasn't too long into our time together that Marc asked one of the questions Abdullah had asked in our living room not too many years before.

"Where are you called?" he asked.

"Iran," I said. I wanted to go where no one else was going.

"Great," he said, and then went on to list three other missionaries who wanted to go to Iran. They were staging in another Central Eurasian country until Iran opened up. I didn't have a peace about going to the country where everyone else was, and I kept praying to God for direction about whether we were supposed to go somewhere else.

Just before we were supposed to leave, some visa problems popped up, so I took the opportunity to voice my concerns to Marc.

"I'm still not convinced God wants us to stage in that country," I said.

"Where do you want to go?" he asked. Marc was so accommodating with us. Whenever we told him we wanted to do something, he was always positive and encouraging. Ann and I laughed because it seemed his response was always, "We can do that!"

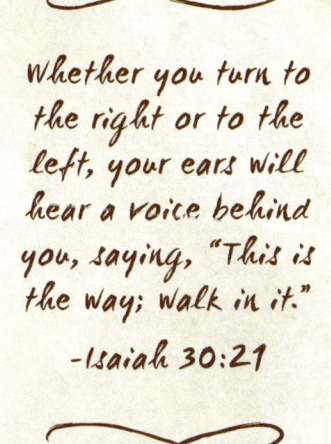

> *Whether you turn to the right or to the left, your ears will hear a voice behind you, saying, "This is the way; walk in it."*
>
> *—Isaiah 30:21*

"I would like to go to a country that borders Iran," I said. "What about Afghanistan or Turkey?"

"How about Istanbul?" he asked.

So we prayed about it as a family, and that's the direction God led us. Our kids were just as excited as we were. Elle saw our journey to Turkey as her own personal adventure, not unlike traveling into Tolkien's Middle Earth or stepping through C. S. Lewis's wardrobe. Both she and Stanley were happy and relieved when the news came that we were approved for Turkey because they also hadn't felt peace with the original plan.

The more I learned about Turkey, the more passionate I became about it. Here was a country of 70 million people with only a few thousand Christians. My expectation was that we would have access to the hard places, the difficult lands, the locations where no one else was going. I wanted to build bridges that would lead to friendships between Christians and Muslims and would open doors to lead Turkish people to Christ.

At our commissioning service the message was based on Psalm 126:5–6:

> *Those who sow with tears*
> *will reap with songs of joy.*
> *Those who go out weeping,*
> *carrying seed to sow,*
> *will return with songs of joy,*
> *carrying sheaves with them.*

The speaker at that service said that if we wanted to reap a harvest, we would have to moisten the dry ground with tears over the lost.

We were willing to go to Turkey and give our lives, not needing to see any fruit but believing that the Lord is faithful. We looked forward to Turkey and prayed for one person to come to Christ, knowing that once that happened we would pray for one more . . . and then one more.

Our mentors, Calvin and Marian Olson, had been pioneer missionaries in Bangladesh for nine years before they saw one convert. They were incredible people of God, and they didn't live to see the thousands in Bangladesh who now follow Christ, but they were faithful to go and do all the Lord asked of them.

When we boarded the plane for Turkey, we expected that, like Calvin and Marian, we would go, work in hard soil, and perhaps never see one person saved. Yet we trusted that one day many Turkish people would come to know Christ as their Savior. We departed for Istanbul on Easter Sunday.

* * * * * *

Within a month of arriving in Turkey, I realized how quickly my personality meshed with the Turks. Our family has a dry sense of humor, which is exactly the sense of humor of the Turkish people. It didn't take long for us to fall in love with the Turks. We put down roots in Istanbul, began studying the language, and started making friends.

My first and closest friend was a man named Baran.

The Turkish people we first met in our neighborhood were so kind. They wanted to help us do everything: whether it was getting our car registered or finding furniture or negotiating our rent price with our landlord. We started asking them questions about the community. The first thing I needed was a cell phone.

"Where can I go to get a cell phone?" I asked in my rudimentary Turkish.

They smiled kindly and directed me to Baran.

"He will help you with all your needs," they said.

But I just need a cell phone, I thought to myself. How much I had to learn!

Decisions here are made as a community, as a family. Later on, when we needed to make some upgrades to our bathroom, many of our Turkish "family" came along to help choose the correct tile. They picked one we didn't particularly like, and it would have been easy for us to overrule their decision. It also would have been very American and doggedly individualistic. But we went with what they chose, and it made them feel even more a part of our lives.

I soon met Baran the cell-phone salesman. A kind-hearted Turkish man with dark hair, dark eyes, and a welcoming smile, he set me up with a cell phone, and I ended up spending hours in his shop, talking with him and listening as other people from the community came and went. We struck a deal: he would teach me Turkish and help me navigate the obstacles that come with being new in the neighborhood, and in return I would teach him English.

Baran quickly became my closest friend, my Turkish brother. I went to his cell-phone shop nearly every day. Although it's only eight feet wide by twelve feet deep, I

> *"Behind this door lives the happiest family in the world."*
> —The Steward Family Motto

realized it was the center of the community. Other middle-aged men who worked in the area would stop by for tea when they had a break. The old men who prayed at the mosque five times a day would come in and sit in one of the three small chairs just inside the door until the next call to prayer. In this way they welcomed me into the community as their brother.

Soon my entire family was under their care. Ann was their sister, Elle and Stanley their niece and nephew. They began inviting us to holiday celebrations and birthday parties, and we reciprocated. Turkey is a culture that loves to celebrate. The people love to visit with neighbors, to spend time with each other, and our apartment soon became a prime meeting place. The neighbors knew that the door to our home was always open to them. We had to buy an industrial-sized teakettle to keep up with the steady stream of visitors. Some evenings we would serve over eighty glasses of tea as various friends from our apartment buildings and the rest of the neighborhood stopped by after work and stayed late into the evening.

One day I went to Baran for some advice on the Turkish language. I always carried a little notebook and pencil around with me, so if I heard something I hadn't heard before I'd write it down and then ask Baran what it meant . . . how it was spelled . . . those kinds of things.

"What do you say to the men in the market after you buy things from them?" Baran asked me. I felt like his English was improving much faster than my Turkish.

I told him how I said thank-you.

He frowned and thought for a moment. Outside it was a beautiful day. They were building a new apartment building across the street, and the noise of the construction mingled with the sound of traffic and the warmth of the sunshine coming down from a blue sky.

"You know," he said, "that works fine, the way you're saying thank-you. But when you're shopping in the market, you really should say it this way."

He said a Turkish phrase. I wrote it down and practiced it.

"Does that sound right?" I asked him.

"Perfect," he said, smiling.

That week when I went into the market, I wandered around and bartered with the vendors as usual. The produce always looked wonderfully fresh, and the nuts and spices were delicious. But that week, after I finished each purchase, I said the phrase Baran had taught me.

By the looks the men gave me, I figured I must not be saying it correctly.

So I went back to Baran's shop and pulled up a chair. He gave me a glass of tea and we talked about what was going on in the community. Outside, cars trudged down the side street. The call to prayer began at the mosque.

"I don't think I'm saying that phrase right," I told him.

"Which phrase?" he asked.

I gave it another try.

"The vendors just look at me kind of funny," I said.

He shook his head.

"It's because you're not accenting the correct syllable," he explained. "You have to say it like this."

I practiced a few more times. *This language is difficult for me*, I thought to myself. But I was determined to fit in, so the next week at the market I went back to the same place and did some shopping. Again the men responded to my farewell statement with strange looks.

I wandered by Baran's shop on my way home that day.

"Baran, I just don't understand," I said. "Whenever I say that phrase, I still get the strangest looks."

Suddenly Baran looked like he was going to burst, and I realized in that instant that I'd been a victim of one of his practical jokes.

"Baran!" I said, shaking my head in disbelief. "What have I been saying?"

He started laughing. Baran tried to hold it in, but it was impossible. Besides, he loves to joke. Soon he was leaning against his counter, practically crying with laughter. Customers came in, but he couldn't even help them.

"Baran!" I said again.

Finally, he managed to talk through the tears.

"Stan, the phrase I taught you doesn't mean thank-you. It actually means . . . 'you have a beautiful behind.'"

For the next few days all of my Turkish brothers stopped me on the street and, using that wonderful Turkish phrase, told me that I had a beautiful behind. Then they'd burst out laughing, and I'd walk away, smiling and shaking my head. Baran won that round.

But not long after he tricked me into using that embarrassing phrase, he asked me to watch his shop while he went down the street to pray. The mosque was only a few yards away, and I didn't mind waiting, so I sat behind the counter while he went out the door. I used my rudimentary Turkish to communicate with the customers who came and went. Then I had an idea.

Just as the prayers were ending, I walked out and stood in front of Baran's shop. People were everywhere, coming in and out of the other stores and walking out to the main road to catch the bus. Just as Baran came out of the mosque and started up the street, he heard me shouting.

"Everything in this shop is free! Everything is free!"

He came running as fast as his legs could carry him.

We were even.

* * * * * *

Even though many aspects of the Turkish culture were easy to adapt to, such as their humor and their welcoming nature, others were more difficult. Their culture is so different from ours.

At first I worried about Stanley. He was a small, ten-year-old kid, probably weighed about forty pounds, and was painfully shy. For his entire life we'd been telling him, "Don't talk to strangers," and "Don't take food from strangers," but once in Turkey we had to reverse that message. The Turkish culture is so kind and outgoing towards visitors, and if you don't respond positively to them they're offended.

Plus, in most Islamic cultures young boys are adored. They're taken care of and looked after, held up as the next generation. Everyone wanted to say hello to Stanley or give him candy or be the one who sat beside him on the bus. It didn't take long for me to realize that my fears for Stanley were needless.

Istanbul is crowded with hundreds of small blue buses that prowl the streets. They operate like taxis in that they pick you up when you hail them, but they operate like buses because they have set routes and will drop you off at any point along them. They move in and out of traffic without worrying about what they might brush up against, so the other vehicles usually make way for them.

Our first time on one of these buses was an adventure. They are supposed to seat thirteen but it's more likely there will be thirty-five people crowded into the seats and standing in the aisle, hanging on for dear life as the bus slams to a halt or lurches ahead. Ann, Elle, Stanley, and I nudged our way on to one of these little blue buses. Before we knew it, an old man reached over and pulled Stanley onto the seat beside him. He wore a knit cap and his wrinkled skin was tan, like leather. His broad smile revealed a host of missing teeth. He put his arm around Stanley and talked to him the entire trip. Stanley had no idea what the guy was saying. I had no clue what the guy was saying.

We got off the bus and I was wondering if the situation had overwhelmed Stanley, but he just grinned.

"Well," he said. "I made my first friend in Turkey."

Elle had a more difficult time adapting, especially during that first year. She was thirteen, and we didn't realize it but in Turkey your age is what you will be turning, so when we landed she instantly went from being thirteen years old to fourteen. And then,

> "The apostle Paul did not have to cut or carve his way but simply had to discover the track that God had prepared for his steps from of old. And when he found it, it . . . would be the very pathway for which his character and gifts were most adapted."
>
> —F. B. Meyer

within two weeks of our arrival, she had a birthday and turned fifteen. She went from being a little girl who our Turkish friends could play with, give candy to, and tease, to being a young woman of marriageable age ... untouchable. She couldn't make eye contact with the men, and they weren't supposed to speak to her.

I think that was tough for her, the transition from little girl to woman in such a short span of time. But we were a close family, and every night we debriefed, processed the day, then went into our family altar where we read the Bible together and prayed. The challenges brought us closer together.

Ann, too, had things to learn. She started pulling her hair back in the style of the Turkish women and learned always to walk behind me. In Turkish culture this isn't done to denigrate the woman, but to allow the man to walk ahead of her and protect her. The man clears the way, declaring silently to those who see him that they may not look at his wife or daughters; they may not touch them.

And this was all in Istanbul, where people tend to be more secular than they are out in the villages. It was good practice for us because soon the adventurous spirit God had given me would lead us east, into the sparsely populated and much more conservative Muslim areas of central and eastern Turkey.

My desire had always been summed up rather well by a quote from David Livingstone, "I am ready to go anywhere, provided it be forward." So immediately, as soon as we arrived in Turkey, I felt my heart being drawn to the border areas, those unapproachable mountain regions that run along Iran, Iraq, and Syria. I hadn't heard of any other Christians working in those areas.

I thought we should go, so we asked God about it. What would that look like, simply driving east into the back country of Turkey, traveling the same roads as the shepherds and nomads and warlords? We came to a conclusion: we wouldn't know exactly what it would look like, but we knew it was where God was leading us—we made plans to head east.

We stopped by the ruins of an ancient church along the Silk Road.

Scan this code to watch a video introduction to this chapter.

CHAPTER 9

OUR FIRST SILK ROAD EXPEDITION

"Certainty of death, small chance of success, what are we waiting for?!"
FROM *THE LORD OF THE RINGS: THE RETURN OF THE KING*

AS WE LEFT ISTANBUL behind and drove into the wilderness of central and eastern Turkey, on what we eventually called our Silk Road Expeditions, I thought back to when I was a boy. I remembered climbing the Liquid Amber tree in our front yard. I usually did it on one of the few fall days in El Cajon. I would put on a flannel shirt, jeans, and a leather belt that held a WWII ammunition pouch with my knife inside.

I worked my way up as high as I could go, branch by branch. The bark scratched my hands and the earth was a long, long way below me. Then, close to the top, I carved my initials and the date into the bark and looked out towards the surrounding mountains. I always had the frontier in mind, even at that young age. It was a

John Wayne kind of desire. If no one had been there, I wanted to go. If someone had already been there, I had to find a new place to go.

That same desire sums up my personal missionary theology: go where no other Christians are going. Often, people ask me how to begin a ministry like ours, but I'm not sure there's a formula you can follow.

If people ask why we do what we do, I tell them that our dedication has always been to the community we are in. Every decision we make is community focused. You're known by the folks you associate with, so if I'm always hanging out with other missionaries or spending a lot of my time with other Americans, the Turkish people will look at me and say, "He's an American living among the Turks."

> *It has always been my ambition to preach the gospel where Christ was not known, so that I would not be building on someone else's foundation.*
> —Romans 15:20

On the other hand, if only once every two or three months we visit other Americans and our family goes to our Turkish friends' birthday parties and religious observances frequently, then people say, "They are Turks." We told our missionary country leaders when we first arrived that we wanted to invest our time in developing friendships with the local people so we were going to limit the time we spent with the rest of the missionary team to a few times a year. We wanted to be welcomed into the Turkish community—we had that desire deep in our hearts.

Our instinct always told us to delve deeper into the Turkish culture. So when we arrived in Istanbul and saw how Western it was, we knew we wanted to go out into the areas of the country with less Western influence. We wanted to be in a place where the people had never had a chance to hear the gospel. Istanbul was a massive city with millions who indeed did not know who Jesus was, but the city had churches—not many, but they were there. We felt led to engage the unreached in a place where there were absolutely no Christians and no knowledge of what a Christian was. So we started driving east … as far as we could go.

The first time we got a rental car and started out on a Silk Road Expedition (SRE), we headed for a town that bordered Iran. (I'll leave the name of the town out in order to protect the identity of some of the people who befriended us there.) It was about 800 miles as the crow flies, perhaps 1,200 miles by road. During our first seven years in Turkey, we probably drove that stretch—the length of the country—forty times.

The roads have improved slightly, but in our earlier days it was tough going. Within our first term, the youth of our denomination raised enough money through their amazing missionary vehicle program and gave us a four-wheel-drive truck. That helped us get into even more remote places, villages that had been completely beyond our reach. Without that truck, we could never have made so many trips or prayed with so many people.

On that first trip, we chose a particular town at the eastern edge of Turkey as our destination because it's in a part of Turkey that juts into Iran—and it's as east as we can go! And, as we soon discovered, it's a gun-running, dope-smuggling, human-trafficking hub patrolled by tanks instead of police cars. It's a powder keg.

So when this little American family showed up in a 4X4, we had to keep our sense of humor. When we first entered this town, we were on the receiving end of some hard, Turkish stares. A Middle-Eastern stare can be a daunting thing! But early on I used some phrases that helped.

"Hi, my name is Stan and my Turkish sucks."

That usually got them laughing and eased the tension. We learned early on that it was important to diffuse the tension in these situations as quickly as possible. When soldiers or other people who questioned our motives approached the truck I always lowered my windows so they could immediately see into the back seat where Elle and Stanley were sitting. Having our two children along helped. When soldiers see that you're traveling with your family, their suspicions drop. They realize that you're not CIA and you're not there to steal their daughters. Plus, their curiosity is aroused. They want to know who you are and why you would drive into such remote villages.

And it always helped to joke with them, because the Turkish people love to laugh. That's why we meshed so well with them. They look for a reason to laugh—I've never met another people group that wants to find common ground more than the Muslim people in Turkey.

*****

Originally our goal was to drive the entire Silk Road, all the way to China. But when we got to the Turkish border regions and understood how lost the people there were, it overwhelmed us. That part of the country contains thousands of villages, maybe tens of thousands, and few, if any, of the people have ever heard the gospel. They've never had one single hope of running into a Christian.

That village at the far eastern edge of Turkey was a rough, rough town. Half of the streets were mud and the other half were cobblestone. Some of the buildings were fairly modern, but interspersed among them were huts and houses made out of canvas and sheet metal. At one point we took a photo of one of our side-view mirrors: an armored vehicle rumbled along behind us. It looked like a cross between a hummer and a tank, with a turret that had two guns and a spotlight on it. We just kept driving, slowly, and eventually it turned off on another road.

Ann felt impressed that we should stay in that town, but it felt so dangerous that she wanted God to confirm it to the rest of us. So we left the town and headed south towards other villages along the Iranian border. As we drove, we continued to pray, *Lord, guide us. Lead us to where you want us to be.*

One day's drive from that dangerous village we pulled into a gas station and the attendant mistakenly filled our diesel tank with gasoline, so we were stuck. They would have to empty the tank and replace some filters, which put a quick halt to our travels. At first it was frustrating, but I also knew that God can use these kinds of opportunities to lead us. So I turned to the kids.

"Some people like to live within the sound of church and chapel bell; I want to run a rescue shop within a yard of hell."
—C. T. Studd

"I want you guys to pray, okay? Pray about why we're stopped here. Let's find out what God has to say."

It wasn't long before little Stanley piped up.

"I think God wants us to go back to that rough town, where we were yesterday."

We were all silent for a moment. It had been a difficult place, especially for Elle. The culture in Istanbul had been a huge adjustment for her, but in that border town it was oppressive: both she and Ann had to be covered from head to foot and their voices weren't even supposed to be heard. At one point a man had helped us carry our bags to the trunk, and without thinking Ann had said, very quietly, "Thank you." The man had looked at her as if she had cursed him.

Elle remained quiet at Stanley's suggestion. So while we listened carefully to what he had to say, we decided to wait before making any final decision. The hours passed slowly as we waited for the repairs to be made to the truck.

That night we stayed in a hotel infested with earwigs. They squirmed on the ceiling, and when we pulled the covers back they scattered. It was nasty. I barely slept, caught up in thoughts of where God wanted us to go next. But the following morning, after the truck had been repaired, Elle came to us with a new revelation.

"I felt the same thing as Stanley," she said quietly. "I felt like we should go back to that town, but I didn't want to. It's so spiritually dark. But I know that's where we're supposed to go."

So I called back to the town and spoke with a few of the people we had met.

"We're coming back," I said. "Is there a place we can stay?"

The greeting we received when we returned was amazing. Before, when Elle or Ann spoke in the presence of a man, the people bristled. But when we went back, the people I'd spoken with on the phone came out and smiled and shook my hand. They couldn't have been friendlier or more welcoming. I think they were impressed that we'd come back. They played with Stanley and helped us look for a place to live.

"How much would an apartment cost?" I asked. The guy from the hotel pulled a rack of keys out from his desk, walked us down the street, and showed us an apartment. It would cost $110 per month, and every window in the place looked out towards the beautiful peaks of Mt. Ararat. It was unbelievable!

> Enlarge the place of your tent, stretch your tent curtains wide, do not hold back; lengthen your cords, strengthen your stakes. For you will spread out to the right and to the left; your descendants will dispossess nations and settle in their desolate cities.
>
> —Isaiah 54:2-3

God had planted us squarely in the middle of one of the most dangerous towns in the region. This would be our eastern base. I couldn't stop staring out the windows. The town was at 6,000 feet above sea level, and towering above our sixth floor apartment was Mt. Ararat, rising to 18,000 feet.

God knew I was an adventurer, and He had led us to one of the most adventuresome places in Turkey—one of the most dangerous places in Turkey. For the first time in my life, I felt like

I was right in the middle of God's calling for my life. I couldn't wait to see what would happen next.

OUR FIRST SILK ROAD EXPEDITION

Spending time with a nomadic tribesman.

Scan this code to watch a video introduction to this chapter.

CHAPTER 10

KINDNESS FROM THE TURKISH PEOPLE

"I hope we will always have mavericks in our denomination. Without them, we'll become very bland. We need people who occasionally, in a right spirit, kick against the traces and forge new paths!"

GEORGE O. WOOD

THE LANDLORD WHO owned the apartment complex where we moved also lived at the top of the building, in the unit just above ours. His apartment took up half the footprint of the seventh floor, and the other half was a miniature mosque, something called a *mescit*. The views into Iran from that terrace were magnificent.

He was a Kurd, and there was friction between Kurds and Turks. Every time I met with him, he seemed to be surrounded by a lot of stern-faced men. Soon I realized they were his entourage. He traveled around in a beautiful Mercedes that had dark windows and pleated curtains surrounding his seating area. He always wore a long black cape, and when he got out of his car someone opened the door for him and the cape would kind of swirl around him. He wore large, dark sunglasses. I started to wonder what kind of stuff he was into.

He looked like a stereotypical Arab from the 70s with those huge sunglasses. In his office I saw pictures of him with his family, and even in the studio portraits he wore the sunglasses. I could tell he was a man who carried a lot of influence. Every once in a while, when we went up to our apartment, we would pass him. He was always kind and loving to us, greeting me with a kiss on both cheeks.

* * * * * *

One day I was out working on the truck, and Ann went to do some shopping. Stanley and Elle went with her. Without me along, Ann still needed male representation, and even though Stanley was only ten years old he could fill that role.

So I worked down there on the street, buried under the hood of the truck. Every so often one of those armored vehicles would drive by, clattering and rumbling on the cobblestone. It was a busy town. A few hours later Ann came back.

"Where's Stanley?" she asked.

"I don't know," I said. "He was with you, wasn't he? I haven't seen him."

"He came over here twenty minutes ago to be with you."

I looked at her.

"Are you sure?" I asked.

She nodded. I could tell by the look in her eyes she was trying not to panic.

"I didn't see him," I repeated, but by then we were already looking up and down the street. Where would a ten-year-old boy be in a town like that, where the police carried automatic weapons and patrolled the streets in tanks?

We raced into our apartment building. There was no electricity that day—the electricity and the water went off all the time—so we walked up the dark stairwell using the light from my flip-up cell phone. The elevator wasn't working, and we were on the sixth of seven floors. I hoped that we'd run into Stanley somewhere in the stairwell. Maybe we'd crossed paths and he was coming back out to look for us. But we didn't see him.

We got up to our apartment, but immediately we knew he wasn't inside. We always left our shoes by the door, and his shoes weren't there—besides, the door was locked. Still, we went in and made sure. We checked all of the rooms. No Stanley.

We walked back out into the hallway. The place was dark, with only a small amount of light trickling in through dusty windows. I tried not to think about all the worst-case scenarios that could happen to a ten-year-old boy in a town on the border between Turkey and Iran. We were just about to head back down the stairwell and begin

> "God's presence was with us even in the most dangerous places in the world. I would never want to go to those places on my own strength, but because God led us there, we were confident and at peace."
>
> —Stan

searching the streets when Ann pointed down the hall towards our neighbor's doorway.

Then I saw them: Stanley's small boots, outside an apartment, three doors down. We'd never met the people who lived there. We walked quickly down the hall and knocked on the door.

The woman who answered wore a blue-gray dress and a white head scarf that covered everything except her face. She had kind, dark eyes, olive skin and smiled in a way that didn't reveal any of her teeth. She acted as if she'd been expecting us.

"Is my son here?" Ann asked, struggling for composure.

"Yes, yes! Come in."

And there was Stanley, sitting calm as can be, drinking warm juice and eating hazel nuts—neither of which he liked but he knew the culture and appreciated the woman's kindness.

The woman spoke to us in Turkish.

"He came up to your door, and he was alone so I brought him in here—that way I could watch over him until you came back."

When she found him on the doorstep, she instantly brought him in, gave him juice, fed him nuts, and turned on the television. She loved him. Her family loved him. She was Kurdish, so her Turkish had a strong accent, but it didn't matter because we had only been there eight months and Stanley couldn't speak Turkish at that point anyway.

> Jesus replied, "Let us go somewhere else—to the nearby villages—so I can preach there also. That is why I have come."
>
> —Mark 1:38

Once again we were overwhelmed by the hospitality of the Turkish people. There Stanley was, a little boy walking in a dark hallway and an elderly neighbor saw him and took him in and cared for him until we got back.

Who are these people? I wondered. *And where does this kindness come from?*

* * * * * *

Years earlier, back in the States, we'd lived close to the border town of Tijuana, Mexico, and it was a rough little town, a seedy kind of place. But it was nothing compared to that border town where our apartment looked out on Mt. Ararat. That place was dark, and dangerous. I was always on high alert. But I also knew that God had taken us there for a reason, so I wasn't afraid.

One night by our truck, I waited for the satisfying click of the locks before walking away. The streets were quiet and Mt. Ararat rose up, piercing a jet-black sky. A shopkeeper I'd gotten to know walked by just as I locked the truck. He stopped and looked at me. "Oh, you don't have to do that," he said, smiling.

I don't have to lock my truck in this town? Are you kidding me? I thought to myself.

"Why is that?" I asked, grinning, expecting him to come back with some kind of joke or one-liner.

"Because you're under his protection," he said.

I gave him a quizzical look, and he pointed up towards the top of our apartment building, this time with a serious expression on his face, before he turned and walked away.

It turns out that our landlord, the man who had rented the apartment to us and lived on the seventh floor directly above us, was a local warlord, extremely powerful in that region of Turkey. We could go anywhere we wanted in that border town of around 55,000 people, and we would be safe because everyone knew we were under his protection.

It was a miracle of God. Instead of choosing a righteous man, God put us under the protection of a warlord, the guy behind most of the "questionable activities" going on in that area. He had access to weapons, manpower, and all kinds of illegal trade. But God gave us supernatural favor, and he loved our family. He protected us.

Later some friction developed between him and the Turkish government. We got a call from one of his representatives from the border town during the winter while we were living in Istanbul.

"Are you going to be living here exclusively or will you still be splitting your time between here and Istanbul?" they wanted to know.

"We'll still be spending the winters in Istanbul," I said.

"Then it's probably best if you don't stay in our town at all. The government is coming down hard on us, and we don't want it to negatively affect you. If you're seen as close friends with us, they might come down on you, too."

Sadly, we didn't go back to that town. But God had other towns and villages He couldn't wait to show us.

Enjoying the view in the eastern region of Turkey near Mt. Ararat.

Scan this code to watch a video introduction to this chapter.

CHAPTER 11
GOD'S HAND OF PROTECTION

Do not go where the path may lead. Go instead where there is no path and leave a trail.
RALPH WALDO EMERSON

DURING ONE OF OUR expeditions, when we'd only been in the country for a year and a half, we found ourselves traveling along the border of Iran and Turkey again. As we continued on the road, it eventually led us on long stretches into Iraq and back out again—the only way we knew this was because our GPS kept going back and forth between Turkey and Iraq. We were on a dirt road, one lane wide, surrounded by rough and rocky terrain.

This particular road was closed to civilians, but God had opened a door for us to drive on it, so we just kept visiting villages along the way. Some were tiny clusters of ramshackle homes built on the steep hillsides. They were constructed with handmade brick or concrete block, intermingled with walls of corrugated steel held together by wood planks. All around them, the hillsides were covered in hardy shrubs and small trees. Farther up the hill I could see north-facing, shadowy slopes still covered in a thin layer of snow. Beyond the hill on which the town was built, far off in the distance, snow-capped mountains reached up into the sky.

Other villages were so large they felt more like bustling cities. But even their main roads were often dirt, and filled with the dust kicked up by the vehicles. The houses were a strange mishmash of old and new, with air conditioning units and satellites mounted on the sides, built of plywood or more corrugated steel. Ladders propped against the houses provided entrance to the second floor. Some windows were glass while others had been boarded over. Huge power lines rose outside the village, then raced off to the west, to civilization.

The people's kindness continued to overwhelm us. We'd enter the villages and the people, who worked hard to care for their families, would give us tea and feed us a meal—sometimes giving us all they'd prepared for dinner. I hated to eat it because I knew it meant they would go without, but it would've been a great offense to say no. We ate the food and sometimes, when there

> "LORD, you alone are my portion and my cup; you make my lot secure. The boundary lines have fallen for me in pleasant places; surely I have a delightful inheritance. I will praise the LORD, who counsels me; even at night my heart instructs me. I keep my eyes always on the LORD. With him at my right hand, I will not be shaken."
>
> —Psalm 16:5-8

wasn't enough, they sat and watched us eat, smiling and asking if we wanted more.

We entered a portion of that road, about 150 miles in distance. Heat billowed up in waves off of the dusty wilderness. As we came around a sharp bend in the road, we encountered a large truck in front of us. It wasn't quite a semi, but it was a huge cargo truck, and it was parked to the side of the road and blocking all traffic. The engine was shut off, which seemed strange to me.

I got out of our vehicle and walked up to the truck. I found the driver sitting quietly in his seat.

"What's going on?" I asked.

The man was sweating. His truck was just parked there, and even though he had his windows down it had to have been well over a hundred degrees in the cab. He leaned out towards me and looked very serious.

"Get back in your truck!" he said, gesturing wildly towards the road in front of us. "There are land mines everywhere! During the night, Iraqi terrorists came up and seeded the road with land mines."

"How long until we can get through?" I asked.

"It could be hours."

I looked up the road. All day that road had felt distant and secluded, but now . . . it felt downright ominous. What was hidden under the dirt?

"Okay," I said. "We'll just turn around and drive back to the last village and stay there for the night. I guess they'll have it cleared up by morning."

"No! You can't do that!" he almost shouted. "You've driven past land mines just getting here. The army is working from the east and the west clearing the mines, from both ends of this long road. They will meet in the middle, somewhere close to here. You need to get back into your truck and turn the engine off so the rumble doesn't trigger a detonation."

"Really?" I was incredulous . . . and beginning to feel a bit apprehensive.

"Yes. We have to wait right here. Please don't drive anywhere! It's not safe!"

So I went back to the truck, turned it off, and explained the situation to Ann and the kids. It was a stifling, hot August day, probably 105 degrees. Ann and Elle were completely covered, wearing head coverings and long tunics. The head covering is a scarf that wraps all the way around a woman's head and can be pulled up in the front to cover her nose and mouth, leaving only her eyes exposed. Their tunics where long and tan, sort of like robes, and they wore them over their normal clothes.

To say it was hot and uncomfortable in that truck is an understatement. But we waited. There was nothing else we could do. The air was filled with an intense silence. Every once in a while dust billowed across the road. I looked up warily at the surrounding mountains and gorges and rock formations. It wouldn't have surprised me to see terrorists appear at any moment.

A few hours later, the military came up behind us and passed by. A few more vehicles joined us in line, parked, and waited. Suddenly we heard an explosion. Then news came back. The road had been cleared. A mine had been discovered only one kilometer in front of us, in the middle of the road. The road wasn't that wide—two cars couldn't pass each other except in select spots. We probably would've hit that land mine had the truck driver allowed us to continue on ahead of him.

I got out of our truck and walked up to the truck driver who'd warned us.

"Thanks for stopping us," I said. "Can I ask a favor? Since it's getting late, would you let me pass you?"

I didn't want to follow in the dust of his truck for the next 100 miles.

Again he became very concerned.

"No, no," he said. "I can't do that. I have to drive in front of you. We don't know how many land mines are still in the road. The military may have missed some. My truck is heavier, so if there are any mines left, I will detonate them. My truck might be able to absorb the blast . . . and in any case . . . I couldn't stand to watch you and your family hit a mine in front of me. I will go ahead and clear the way."

He pulled out and we followed him, passing slowly by the crater where the land mine had been detonated. It was massive. A land mine that size would've torn our truck to pieces!

For the next hundred miles we crept along in his dust. His love for a foreign American family was so great that he couldn't let us go in front. He refused to put our safety at risk.

We finally came to a junction where the dirt road connected with an asphalt road. He honked as we passed by, and we beeped our horn back at him and waved. It brings me to tears every time I think of the kindness of that man.

* * * * * *

The road slowly got better as we headed west. That night we were hot and tired. We'd been sitting in the car for hours, and all the

> *"The kindness of the Turkish people constantly challenges our level of hospitality. They have welcomed us, complete foreigners, as family. They constantly provide us with support and friendship. It makes me wonder about our ingrained, American sense of self-sufficiency, and whether or not that's consistent with the message of Scripture."*
>
> —Stan

dust from the road had mixed with our sweat and covered us in a fine layer of filth. All we wanted was a decent room with a shower, so we stopped at the first little town we came to.

Stanley and I walked inside, but then we realized it wasn't really a hotel. It was more like a large house that rented out rooms. We went up to the desk.

"Can I see a room?" I asked.

The guy took me upstairs. There was something wrong with the windows. Either they didn't have glass in them or they didn't shut properly. But whatever the case, dirt and sand filled the room. A stiff breeze blew in and occasionally whipped all of that dust up into a frenzy. It was a tiny space and the kids would've had to sleep on the floor. That wasn't uncommon, but after the stressful day we'd been through, I had hoped that all of us could get a good night's rest.

Stanley was the youngest and the most tired, so I left the choice up to him.

"Do you want to stay here or keep looking?" I asked, then warned him, "I don't know if we'll find anything better in the next town."

"Let's keep looking," he said.

So we drove down the road. Elle and Stanley sat silently in the back. Ann looked out the passenger window. It was hard to believe that just that morning we'd been sitting on a dusty road waiting for the military to clear land mines. After an hour or so another little town came into view on the horizon.

We followed a tank into town as it patrolled the streets with a spotlight searching for terrorists. There we found exactly what we'd been hoping for: a decent hotel with a shower, a restaurant, and an air conditioner blowing lukewarm air. Dinner that night tasted like the first food we'd eaten in years. The four of us filled up, then went to our room and took wonderful, hot showers without even caring about the water leaking from the shower across the bathroom floor. What a day. What a night.

The next morning we went down to the lobby to check out and noticed a television showing Turkish news. The station was broadcasting live video from a small town where a minibus had been stopped by armed gunmen who then strafed the bus with machine-gun fire. They had killed thirteen people.

As the shot widened out from the bullet-riddled, torn up minibus, something came into view—a house. Suddenly, I realized the minibus was parked in front of the little place where we'd stopped the night before . . . the place where, after looking at the room, Stanley had said, "Let's keep looking."

How closely God watched over us!

※ ※ ※ ※ ※ ※

There were several instances during that trip where we went through controlled checkpoints. We'd pull up to a little guard station and there'd be a wooden arm blocking the road. Young men with guns would come out and surround the truck, usually searching it for weapons or contraband.

But once they saw Stanley, they smiled. Sometimes they'd get a soccer ball out and he'd play with them. Other times they let him hold their weapons or they'd give him a tour of their tanks. At one checkpoint we took a picture of Stanley with three of the guards. They were young men, maybe twenty, wearing green fatigues, black boots, and kind smiles. They all had short, black hair and a few days of stubble on their chins. One of them put his arm around Stanley, who grinned from ear to ear under the wide brim of his baseball cap.

Shortly after we left those checkpoints, they were attacked by terrorists and every soldier was killed. Those young men with the smiling faces and kind eyes? Gone. God had His hand of protection over us, but it was heart-breaking because even though we were protected, the people behind us were attacked and killed. All along, the love of the Turks surrounded us. They went in front of us and protected us when it was needed. It was an amazing thing to experience.

I often wonder about the way we treat foreigners when we run into them in America. Do we love them? Would we drive our truck ahead of them to absorb a land mine? Or do we do all that we can to get them out of our hair as quickly as possible?

We learned a lot about the Turkish culture during those first few years: the warmth in their hearts for visitors, their overwhelming hospitality, and their love of laughter. But we were also keenly aware of the darkness of their religion and their need for Christ. As our first two or three years in Turkey passed, we realized it would take much more to reach them. But we weren't sure what that was.

Meanwhile, God used those first few years to begin leading us to a new area of the country that we should focus on: a place called the Dark Canyon.

Stanley crossing the Bosporus
in Istanbul.

CHAPTER 12
TRAVELING ON THE SILK ROAD

"I looked for someone among them who would build up the wall and stand before me in the gap on behalf of the land so I would not have to destroy it, but I found no one."

EZEKIEL 22:30

THERE ARE FOUNTAINS scattered everywhere throughout Istanbul, washing fountains where men perform ablutions prior to going into the mosque. The water in the fountains is always running. Washing before prayer is a vital aspect of the Islamic culture. It's listed as a requirement, but most of the people I know wash less for its requirement and more for its mystical, spiritual aspects.

As I learned to speak Turkish, I tried to discover the verb root to the Turkish word *ablution*. I found I could learn a lot about how the Turks view a particular action if I knew what the root of the verb meant.

"When you do your ablutions, are you *making* ablutions or *doing* ablutions? How does that work?" I asked.

> *"I think about all the people I hope will read this book. I think about your lives and how God wants to use you. I think about how His perfect plan always resonates with the deepest desires of our hearts. Who are you called to?"*
>
> —Stan

The answer was a great doorway into the Muslim mind: they "take" their ablutions. In other words, when they wash, the Turkish verb root implies that they are "taking" their cleansing from Allah. This showed a great cultural awareness for the need to be cleansed. I began to pray every day that my Turkish brothers and sisters would find this cleansing through the Son of God, Jesus Christ.

Istanbul wasn't the only place in Turkey with fountains—they were everywhere, often in the most unlikely places. We washed in some beautiful fountains on our travels, and we washed in some humble ones. It's difficult to explain the amazing feeling you get when you find an old fountain along a dirt road, probably hundreds of years old and built for shepherds or nomadic tribesmen, with spigots of water that run twenty-four hours a day. You take your shoes off at the end of a long, hot drive and wash your head and your hands and your neck, running water through your hair. It's incredibly refreshing!

These experiences reminded me so much of the New Testament, when Jesus washed people's feet. I think about the comment He made in Luke 7:44–48 (NLT):

> Then [Jesus] turned to the woman and said to Simon, "Look at this woman kneeling here. When I entered your home, you didn't offer me water to wash the dust from my feet, but she has washed them with her tears and wiped them with her hair. You didn't greet me with a kiss, but from the time I first came in, she has not stopped kissing my feet. You neglected the courtesy of olive oil to anoint my head, but she has anointed my feet with rare perfume."
>
> "I tell you this, her sins—and they are many—have been forgiven, so she has shown me much love. But a person who is forgiven little shows only little love." Then Jesus said to the woman, "Your sins are forgiven."

In Bible times there was something sacred about giving someone water to wash with. There was something intimate, something compassionate about such an offer. But I think there's also something hidden in this passage that many people miss: Jesus placed a value on tears. He said that the man didn't give him water to wash his feet, but he also pointed out that the woman washed them with her tears.

I think there's value in our sorrows, especially when we place them at the feet of Jesus. God has been teaching me the importance of this. Don't squander your sorrows.

✶ ✶ ✶ ✶ ✶ ✶

I wrote a series of articles about our trips into eastern Turkey. We called them Silk Road Expeditions. I tried to write from a secular perspective, simple travel logs from an area of the world that's rarely visited. I sent writings to various newspapers and travel sites.

In a region where missionary activity is illegal, these articles gave us a "reason" to be able to travel in such remote areas. Soon it became what we were known for. We stopped in villages and told them that we wanted to write about their village, that we wanted to get to know their history, and we'd stay there and become friends with the people. We shared their stories in print, stories about what it's like to live in those areas of Turkey, what their hopes and dreams are, and the way of life their children have and hope to attain. But even more important, whenever we left a village, we asked if we could pray with them.

My desire to keep going to more and more remote places never faded, and travel writing brought opportunities to visit places that might have been closed to us otherwise. Over the years we continually passed by this "triangle of terrorism" in south-central Turkey. It was occupied by the PKK, the Kurdish rebels. We didn't even say that organization's name without dropping our voices because they were so feared in the region.

This triangle of terror was central to the Kurdish struggle for independence, an ongoing conflict that has claimed 40,000 lives over the past twelve years. This spring, in four or five weeks' time, 115 terrorists were killed and around thirty soldiers and police in the area lost their lives. This triangle is a hotbed for Islamic militants. It's a place most people try to avoid.

Many young people who stay in the region rather than move to the larger cities become targets for indoctrination because of the hopelessness in these dark areas. These are the young men and women who blow themselves up in the name of an extremist cause.

Any time you hear about a suicide bomber, you need to weep not only for the victims but also for the person who strapped on the explosives, likely a young person. It takes a tremendous amount of passion for the truth to be distorted to the point where a nineteen-year-old kid, with all of those years in front of him, will blow himself up ... end his life ... for the sake of a lie he trusts.

But they continue to convince kids to do it.

God put this area of the country on our hearts. Within this triangle is the Euphrates, a river that has always fascinated me. Both the Euphrates and the Tigris begin in Turkey, and they were two of the original rivers that flowed out of the Garden of Eden, so there are some who theorize the Garden of Eden was located in modern day Turkey. Sometimes, when we crested a hill and looked down to see a deep, winding gorge, and then looked out on the horizon and saw massive, snow-capped mountains, it wasn't hard to believe that Eden may have been hidden somewhere close by.

> *He has saved us and called us to a holy life—not because of anything we have done but because of his own purpose and grace. This grace was given us in Christ Jesus before the beginning of time, but it has now been revealed through the appearing of our Savior, Christ Jesus, who has destroyed death and has brought life and immortality to light through the gospel.*
> *—2 Timothy 1:9-10*

Within this triangle, we found a place called the Dark Canyon. The road there clings to the side of the gorge and winds along a cliff that falls down into the Euphrates. The road vanishes in and out of a series of tunnels and arches. During the winter, it's covered in ice—the area gets up to six feet of snow during colder months.

This Dark Canyon used to be an ancient shortcut, a part of Turkey where the original Silk Road passed by. The road has been there for a thousand years and passes through village after village after village. In every single one, there is a mosque, a fountain, and an imam. In every village the call to prayer is issued five times a day. Very few of the people in those villages have ever heard of the gospel. They all need someone to come alongside them, to share the Good News with them. But it's not going to be reached in a week or two, or even a year or two. I think of Abdullah and the way that he challenged me that night in San Diego, twenty years ago. I remember the look on his face and the way his finger thudded against my chest.

I remember the questions he asked me.

Are you called?

Who are you called to?

The interior of a mosque.

CHAPTER 13

THE SIGN OF THE DOVE

Do not be anxious about anything, but in every situation, by prayer and petition, with thanksgiving, present your requests to God. And the peace of God, which transcends all understanding, will guard your hearts and your minds in Christ Jesus.

PHILIPPIANS 4:6–7

PRAYING FOR MUSLIMS is vitally important to missionary work, and prayers to Jesus from their homes and meetings places are a direct and powerful form of spiritual warfare.

The prayer times I had for Muslims "on their turf" were some of the most intense prayer times of my life. During those periods of intercession, I prayed: *Dear God, in the men all around me, break down the walls of their hearts right now. Open their eyes, God. Break down the wall of Islam. Demolish this stronghold. Let fountains of truth erupt out of the floor they kneel on. Let fountains of truth flow so that these people will see You and hear You and know You. Immediately, right now, imprint on their hearts and minds the name of Jesus. While* they're praying, visit them supernaturally. Stamp the name of Jesus the Savior on their souls.

We claim this territory by Your blood, and we drive back the forces of Satan. We drive back the darkness. We destroy the strongholds of Satan in the name of Jesus Christ.

I continued praying under my breath and in my spirit, and I wept while I prayed.

I often saw Muslim men weeping while they prayed because of heavy needs in their lives. But from what I understood, the Muslim men I knew did not weep out of a love for Allah. So they would see me weeping and they would think, *Stan must have heavy needs in his life.* And I did have heavy needs. I wept and prayed and pushed my forehead into the prayer rug for them . . . for their souls.

> I have come into the world as a light, so that no one who believes in me should stay in darkness.
> —John 12:46

There are enough of my tears to seed something. I continue to hope that our tears will lead to rivers of life and truth flowing through the streets of Istanbul, and that the river of God's love and truth will grow deeper as it moves out into the countryside. I have to believe that in God's timing and through God's power something will grow from those prayers we planted.

God, be glorified in this place, I often prayed, and I would feel such a heaviness of Satan, such a demonic opposition to us being there that sometimes the only thing I could do was sing under my breath.

Oh, the blood of Jesus!
Oh, the blood of Jesus!
Oh, the blood of Jesus!
It washes white as snow!

Sometimes I couldn't pray and I couldn't sing, so I just said that one phrase over and over again: "The blood of Jesus . . . the blood of Jesus."

I thought back to the way my grandfather had prayed when I was a boy. I remembered lying beside him on the platform at the front of that little church, and I know that being with him at such a young age was preparation for me because in those moments he was teaching me, a five-year-old boy, how to enter into the presence of God . . . how to depend on Him.

Satan does not want us in his territory. He has ruled in Islamic lands for fourteen centuries. But now we're going in, in the midst of his throne, where he sits, and we are praising the name of his enemy, lifting up the name of Christ, singing about the blood of Christ, the blood of Jesus.

As the years passed, I started praying more and more in the Spirit when I was praying with my Muslim friends. There was such a groaning in my soul for those men who kneel and rise and kneel and rise. Some of them go to the mosque five times a day, seven days a week. They would fast during the month of fasting, give to charity, meet dietary restrictions . . . do everything they knew to do. But their hearts were full of darkness, and their spirits weren't right with God. My heart would be so heavy for them, for their salvation that the only way I could pray was in the Spirit.

One Friday, I prayed: *God, I'm so tired. The walk here is a long, spiritually dark journey. It's exhausting me. I don't want to come to this place and be surrounded by the lost without having the opportunity to lead them to You. It's so hard not being able to speak light into their lives.*

God, I need You to visit us while we're here today. I need to know You are with me. That's why I come here, to bring Your presence into the midst of these men. I want to know You are here. I want to know Your Spirit is moving.

At that moment a dove flew in and floated over to where I was praying. It hovered above me for three or four seconds. Everyone kept looking at me, then up at the dove, then back at me again.

Then the dove flew off.

That was God's moment for me.

I AM HERE. I AM WITH YOU.

> "There's something about praying as a family that's so powerful. There's something about the experience of having a grandfather or a mother or an uncle or a father show you how to pray that will stay in your mind as long as any other memory."
>
> —Stan

THE SIGN OF THE DOVE

Stanley and a Turkish friend.

CHAPTER 14
THE GIFT OF GOD'S WORD

Christ has no body on earth but yours, no hands but yours, no feet but yours. Yours are the eyes through which Christ's compassion for the world is to look out; yours are the feet with which He is to go about doing good; and yours are the hands with which He is to bless us now.

SAINT TERESA OF AVILA

ONE DAY STANLEY AND I were sitting with Turkish friends.

In Turkey they have a deep appreciation for boys and young men. They understand the importance of the next generation of men and how they will be the ones to shape their culture. My Turkish friends always gravitated to Stanley. When we first arrived they called him their nephew, but now that he's older they call him "brother."

So anyway, Stanley ended up sitting with some men separated from me. An imam joined the group wearing a formal outfit made of beautiful ivory cloth with scarlet lining and a special cap. He swept in and walked toward the front, through the crowd. But there was no aisle, so as the men sensed him coming behind them they leaned to the side and created a place for him to walk. He usually walked straight up the middle of the room.

But on that day the imam saw my son sitting quietly among the crowd, and he skewed off on a diagonal course so he could pass by Stanley. This created a small amount of pandemonium, because suddenly no one knew where the Imam was going. Men shifted this way and that, trying to create a walking space, but some of them ended up leaning into his path. He had to slow down and gently nudge some of the men aside.

> *May the God of peace . . . equip you with everything good for doing his will, and may he work in us what is pleasing to him, through Jesus Christ, to whom be glory for ever and ever. Amen.*
>
> —Hebrews 13:20-21

The imam walked up behind Stanley, put his hands on his shoulders, leaned down and kissed him on the top of his head. I felt immensely proud of my son in that moment. He had always carried himself with such humility among these Muslim men, respecting their traditions and their ways.

Then the imam said something in a low voice that I couldn't hear. I asked Stanley what the imam had said, but he couldn't quite understand him either.

This happened numerous times over the course of several months, and I could never quite hear the imam. He would veer through the crowd, altering his course from the middle of the room, and place his hands on Stanley's shoulder, kiss the top of his head, then say a few short sentences.

One day I sat on the floor close enough to Stanley so that when the imam stopped and put his hands on Stanley's shoulders and kissed the top of his head, I finally understood what he had been saying.

"Men of Turkey . . . men of Islam, here a Christian and his son worship God. Where are our sons?"

* * * * * *

By the time 2009 rolled around, it was time for us to return to the States on furlough. I always hated to leave our community, especially for a year at a time, but I knew it was important for us to reconnect with friends and family in the States. Sometimes it's a difficult balance to achieve, that line between living out our calling but also spending the time to cast the vision to others.

So as we prepared to leave, I wondered what I could do for the imam who'd been so kind to us, who'd welcomed Stanley and I into his community, and allowed us to pray to Jesus there. I felt such a deep appreciation that he was willing to publicly say, "You may come among us and pray to Jesus." Then I had an idea.

I'd obtained an Arabic Bible, a special edition that was beautifully ornate. It included both the Old and New Testaments. This imam was highly trained, as are most imams in Turkey, and even though he's Turkish by birth he reads, speaks, and studies in Arabic. On our last day in the community before leaving on furlough, Stanley and I took this Bible to give to the imam as a gift.

Muslims treat their holy books with the utmost respect—they are always stored in high places, close to the Koran. You would never find anyone laying the Koran on a seat, much less on the floor. If you go into a Muslim's house, you'll always find the Koran on the highest shelf.

I felt unsure how to present this Bible to the imam. I didn't want to miss an opportunity, but I also didn't want to give him the Bible if it wasn't God's timing. This wasn't meant to be a fundraising exercise, an action that would allow me to go back to the States and raise money based on the fact that we were giving Bibles to Muslims. I wanted the imam to accept it within the framework of our friendship, with respect on both sides. I wanted it to be an anointed gift, given at an anointed time, for an anointed purpose.

I marveled at the depth of the relationships God had given to us in the community, and I truly felt like these beloved Turks were my family, my brothers. I prayed that God would keep them until we could return and continue showing them Christ's love.

Everyone wanted to have their picture taken with us, so it was a long but fun farewell. At the end, after most of the group had trickled out onto the streets and headed back to home or work, the imam came over to Stanley and I. He seemed pleased at the little gathering of people who'd stayed to see us off. He cared a lot about that community and had always been so welcoming to me and my family.

He pulled out an old, worn set of light blue prayer beads and handed them to Stanley. The thirty-three beads were connected in a circle, with two smaller, silver ornaments towards the top. Muslims use prayer beads to pray through the ninety-nine names of Allah, but I use mine to list off the people in my community that I'm praying for.

"These were my father's prayer beads," the imam said solemnly, holding them out towards Stanley. "They're very precious to me. I want you to have them."

I felt my breath escape. What an incredible gift, that of a father to a son! It was an amazing honor for the imam to pass those prayer beads on to Stanley, especially in a culture where the father-son relationship is sacred.

Stanley immediately recognized the value of the gift. Without so much as asking me, he handed the Bible to the imam.

"I want to give this to you," he said in a kind voice. He probably felt a little nervous inside, but his actions and movements spoke only of certainty and love.

The imam reached into the bag and pulled out the Bible, still wrapped in the beautiful paper that Ann had chosen. He gently peeled back the wrapping and stood there, holding the Bible with two hands. What a vision! That was something I'd wanted to see for so long—the Word of God in the hands of one of my Muslim friends.

"What is this?" he asked.

"It's the Word of God," I said solemnly, praying that he would accept it. "It contains the Old Testament and the New Testament."

He nodded, looked at the back then the front again, kissed it, and touched it to his forehead. He looked at Stanley.

"I will cherish this," he said. "I will read this."

At that point one powerful thought went through my mind.

I'm determined to be the one watching this community come to the Lord. God, I'll do anything to see that happen.

These words have resurfaced in my heart during the difficult months we've experienced. When I feel those moments of weakness or doubt, I remember the compassion I felt for this community in that moment when I saw the imam accept the Bible from Stanley and say, "I will read this." I remember what I told God, and it gives me hope and peace: *I will do anything to see this community come to the Lord.*

* * * * * *

The imam gave Stanley the prayer beads on a Sunday. Our flight left on Monday afternoon, so on Monday morning I went by my friend's shop to say good-bye. He welcomed me and tried to convince me to stay for tea, but I rebuffed his offer over and over again and explained that we had to be leaving very soon. He kept shrugging his shoulders and looking at me with reproach, only half joking, but I knew he understood.

He handed me a bag that had about thirty CDs inside it.

"What's all this?" I asked, digging around.

"Those CDs have Islamic music on them . . . some singing and chanting, and also different calls to prayer."

"Really?" I said. "Thank you."

"Oh, they're not from me," he said. "The imam dropped those off for you. It was one last gift he wanted to give you before you went back to the States."

I looked through the bag. I don't know how long it took him to make all those CDs, but he'd labeled each one in his own careful handwriting. Everything was done with great precision and care. That's when I saw what was written on the top of the bag.

Isa.

Isa is the Arabic name for Jesus.

"What does that mean?" I asked my friend. "Why does it say Isa on the top?"

My friend laughed. He seemed a little embarrassed.

"Well," he said, "the imam has a difficult time pronouncing your name. It's not a Turkish name, you know."

We both laughed. The "st" sound at the beginning of a word is unusual, so many of my friends have a hard time saying it.

"When you're not around," he continued, "the only name the imam ever refers to you by is Isa."

His words plowed right over me . . . and left me a quivering mess. I said a hurried good-bye and walked out of the shop as quickly as possible. I couldn't keep back the tears. Walking down that sidewalk in a small community lost in the vastness of Istanbul, I wept. I wept because I was the only Jesus that imam had ever known. I wept because I felt like such a poor copy of Christ, such a poor example. I wept because I thought about how I messed up on a daily basis, and yet I was the one God was choosing to reveal Himself to these wonderful people.

What a powerful reminder to me. Ann, Elle, Stanley, and I were the only representatives of Jesus that our community knew. Even in our faults, even in our failures, even in our daily struggles, we could be Jesus to others. Even as I butchered the Turkish language and lost my temper and displayed my human nature, the

> *Thy word is a lamp unto my feet, a light unto my path.*
> —Psalm 119:105 (KJV)

lost were still somehow, supernaturally seeing Jesus in us. What a God we serve!

Ann and Elle make friends with a village woman.

Scan this code to watch a video introduction to this chapter.

CHAPTER 15
SIGNS AND WONDERS

Before praying "Lord use me," pray "Lord make me usable."
CALVIN OLSON

RECENTLY, IT SEEMS that many Christians, including Ann and I, have started to pray a particular prayer. It's a powerful prayer, even in its simplicity.

Use us, Lord.

At the heart of this prayer is the desire to line up our lives with the lives God has called us to live. I think there's also a longing that our lives wouldn't be wasted, that we wouldn't spend our time here on earth seeking entertainment or pleasure or other things that tend to numb us to the reality of the spiritual realm. It's a challenging prayer because it constantly draws us back into the present and refuses to let us live somewhere off in the future, when things will be better or easier or different.

But it wasn't until recently that Ann and I thought about what that simple prayer really means.

Use us, Lord.

After all, when you use something, it's used up. It's gone. When I use water to wash with, the water does its job and then vanishes down the drain. When I use a pen, eventually the ink runs out. When I use wood to start a fire, the wood is consumed. When we ask God to use us to accomplish His purposes, we're asking Him to wring us out until nothing remains.

> But even if I am being poured out like a drink offering on the sacrifice and service coming from your faith, I am glad and rejoice with all of you.
> —Philippians 2:17

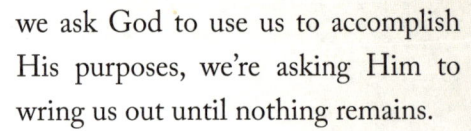

Our prayer became, *Lord, pour us out for these people. Use us. Let us be laid waste for them. We're not looking for an early retirement. We're not looking down the road to life after our twenty years as missionaries—we want to see Muslims saved. This is our life! We want to see our friends find you!*

In 2011, as we continued to pray along these lines, we felt prompted to pray for signs and wonders. We believed that was what it would take to bring Muslims to Christ. Both Ann and I thought that if God moved in a tangible way among our community, if people were healed, if the blind were given sight, if the deaf could hear again, then surely our community would turn to Christ.

Have you ever prayed desperately? Have you ever been so concerned for the souls of your friends and neighbors that the weight of their eternal situation wakes you up at night? There were nights when we couldn't sleep at all because we loved our Turkish family so much and couldn't bear to think about what would happen if any of them passed away without finding Christ.

We prayed desperately for signs and wonders because we believed that's what it would take.

And God answered our prayers.

✶ ✶ ✶ ✶ ✶ ✶

We had a lady living in our apartment building, my Turkish "mother's" mother. She was a tiny little lady in her early eighties, and she'd been diagnosed with terminal cancer. Five large tumors were lodged in her lungs, the dreaded white spots on an x-ray. The surgeons performed a small surgery to remove a portion of her lung, but they soon realized there was nothing they could do to rid her of all of the tumors.

"No chemo," the doctor said, shaking his head sadly. "No radiation. Nothing can help her now. Just take her home and let her die in peace."

In Turkey they don't give the sick person the diagnosis—they only give that to the family members. In the Turkish culture, the doctors don't want to upset the patient, so if there's bad news they'll deliver that to the patient's closest family. Eventually, the patient kind of figures out what's going on, but it can make for some interesting conversations, when you know the person's diagnosis and either they don't know or you're not sure how much they know.

Ann had been going along to all of the doctor's appointments and procedures with these women. Soon after the diagnosis, the woman's daughter, a sixty-year-old woman we refer to as our Turkish "mom," came down to our apartment and spoke to us through her tears. The whole experience with her mother had weighed her down, and she looked exhausted. She hadn't been eating or sleeping well.

"You hear what the doctor is saying," she said in a sad voice. "Will you pray for my mother?"

"Yes," I said. "We will pray."

It's not uncommon for Muslims to say they're praying for you. They do pray to Allah, that his will would be done. Their religion is built around the daily rhythm of prayer. But I felt prompted that day to ask her a question, something I'd never brought up with her before.

"How do you want me to pray?" I asked. "Do you want me to pray to Allah or to Jesus?"

She looked at me, and I felt a strong sense of peace. When you move past the stereotypes and the cultural differences, the national pride and the other things that keep you at arm's length from Muslim people, what you find is a human being with the same desires, doubts, and fears as you. Each one loves their family as dearly as you do. Each one has to navigate a life of everyday worries and eternal questions like you do. Each one is a beautiful individual loved dearly by God.

"Pray to Jesus," she said, nodding her head slightly. "Pray to Jesus."

So I did.

We normally saw their family several times a day. They lived directly above us, and the woman who had cancer stayed with them. She would come down for tea in the morning and the afternoon and the evening, sometimes drifting off to sleep on the little pillows we'd set up on the floor of our living area. But now she was bedridden, so I went up to her apartment every single day. I walked quietly back to her room, and she slowly moved her eyes over and looked at me. She looked like she was fading.

She had these tiny, little feet, probably a size four, and I'd hold them in my hands while I prayed. I thought about that woman washing Jesus' feet with her tears, and I hoped that somehow God would come down and move. I prayed that our tears would move God to compassion for this woman whom we loved. Perhaps she would be the first major healing, the one that would open the eyes of our community to the power of Jesus.

Whenever I prayed for her, I started in Turkish, as well as I could. I prayed in the name of Jesus, and when my Turkish gave out I prayed in English that she would be healed. She was always so thankful that Ann and I took the time to go up to her room and pray for her.

> "You do not need to know precisely what is happening, or exactly where it is all going. What you need is to recognize the possibilities and challenges offered by the present moment, and to embrace them with courage, faith and hope."
> –Thomas Merton

We continued in this way for many, many months. Sometimes other people would join us in the room, and at other times it was just us. I pleaded with God for the miracle we so desperately needed. Finally, eight months after her diagnosis, she went in for a routine checkup. Ann and I thought she looked good—she wasn't bedridden anymore, and her face had life in it.

She visited the doctor and the hospital attendants took an x-ray of her lungs. They seemed to take a long time examining the film before coming back to where we waited.

"The machine is broken," they said abruptly. "We'll have to do an MRI."

You can see where this is heading. After the MRI, they came out with disbelief on their faces. The looked at us as if we were hiding something from them, or perhaps playing some kind of elaborate practical joke.

"The tumors are gone," the doctor said, awe in his voice. "There's nothing in there. She doesn't have cancer."

We were elated. Ann and I thought *this is it! This is what it's going to take to break open the hearts of the Turks.* We returned to our apartment and praised God like never before. Excitement reverberated through the four of us. Elle and Stanley could feel it, too—we were on the verge of something monumental.

But nothing happened. Nothing extraordinary came to pass. We wanted to yell, "Look! Look what God has done!" But we felt God telling us to keep quiet, to let His actions sink into their hearts. So we waited, and the silence weighed heavily on our community. Our neighbors and our Turkish family acknowledged that the healing came after we prayed to Jesus, but it didn't turn their hearts. No souls were saved. Their outlook on religion and Allah led them to a resigned worldview, a sort of shrugging of the shoulders while saying "Thank goodness it was Allah's will that she be healed." They didn't ask questions. No new doorways opened up.

I felt saddened and a little confused by the lack of change.

✶ ✶ ✶ ✶ ✶ ✶

Not long after that, a guy who worked at a store beneath our apartment had a terrible eye infection. The infected eye was always red and constantly watering; it grew steadily worse and more inflamed each day. The infection continued over the course of a couple months, to the point where he was rushed to the emergency room and taken to a special ophthalmology hospital. Everyone thought it was something that antibiotics would take care of, but eventually his doctor broke the bad news to us.

The eye was too far gone to save. There was nothing they could do to repair it. The infection had turned his eye completely white, and he had lost all vision. The doctors placed him in quarantine because he was so infectious; they didn't want to risk anyone else getting it. They decided to wait until the infection subsided before removing the eye because if they performed the surgery now, the bacteria might transfer to his good eye or even to his brain.

Ann and I went to visit him during his three-month quarantine. We walked into the small hospital and asked to see him.

"I'm sorry," the woman said in reception. "You can't go back there. His condition is highly contagious. He's not allowed to have any visitors."

We managed to convince a nurse to take us to him, back through a maze of hallways, past closed doors. We walked into the room. The young man's father sat quietly in a chair beside the bed looking forlorn and lost. The young man looked at us when we walked in. His infected eye was completely opaque.

His Turkish name meant peace. Ann and I walked over to his bedside and we asked how he was doing, what the newest time frames were for surgery.

"We leave tomorrow for our trip," I told him. "We'll be back in one month."

He nodded. I think we were all contemplating the same thing: when Ann and I returned, unless God intervened, his eye would be gone.

"Can we pray for you in the name of Jesus?" I asked.

"Yes," he said.

I prayed for that young man in the name of Jesus, first in Turkish, then in English. I felt God there in that hospital room, and the young man's father had tears running down his cheeks. Once again we begged God, hoping that this blind man receiving his sight would be a miracle that would turn the hearts of our community towards Christ. I fully expected to pull back my hand and see his eye was healed. We finished praying and I looked down at him.

But there was no change. His eye was solid white. I smiled at him, but it was hard not to feel disappointed. I couldn't understand why God wouldn't use this as an opportunity to display His healing power and to bring Muslims to Him. We stayed and talked with the young man and his father for a little bit longer before saying good-bye.

Ann and I left the next day for our one-month trip. I didn't hear anything about the young man while we were away, but when we drove back to our apartment building on New Year's Eve, there he was, standing outside the front door. Ann and I got out and walked towards him. He waved. He was overjoyed.

"Stan," he said. "I can see."

During the month we'd been gone, God had healed his eye and given him 80 percent of his vision back. It was an absolute miracle. We had prayed in the name of Jesus. The people had heard it, and they had witnessed the healing. Jesus was there in the midst of our community, literally giving sight to the blind.

But . . . again . . . nothing changed. There were no new opportunities, no new conversations. No open doors.

What would it take to open the hearts of our Muslim friends? One morning soon after that, I poured my heart out to God.

God, You've performed signs and wonders and healings. But we're not seeing any change in the hearts of our Muslim friends. What will it take? Use us! We're willing to pour ourselves out so the lost will be found.

I was on my knees before God, crying out for the souls of my Muslim neighbors. I told Him, again, that we would do anything it took to turn them towards Him. And then God answered.

The words He gave brought a certain heaviness. I think, in my spirit, I knew immediately what it would take to see a change in our Turkish community. Wonders and healings wouldn't do it. Simply living among them in their community wouldn't be enough. It would take something deeper than that, something more difficult. God's words echoed in my heart for the days, weeks, and months to follow: *Sometimes works of sorrow, loss, and sacrifice speak louder than works of signs, wonders, and miracles.*

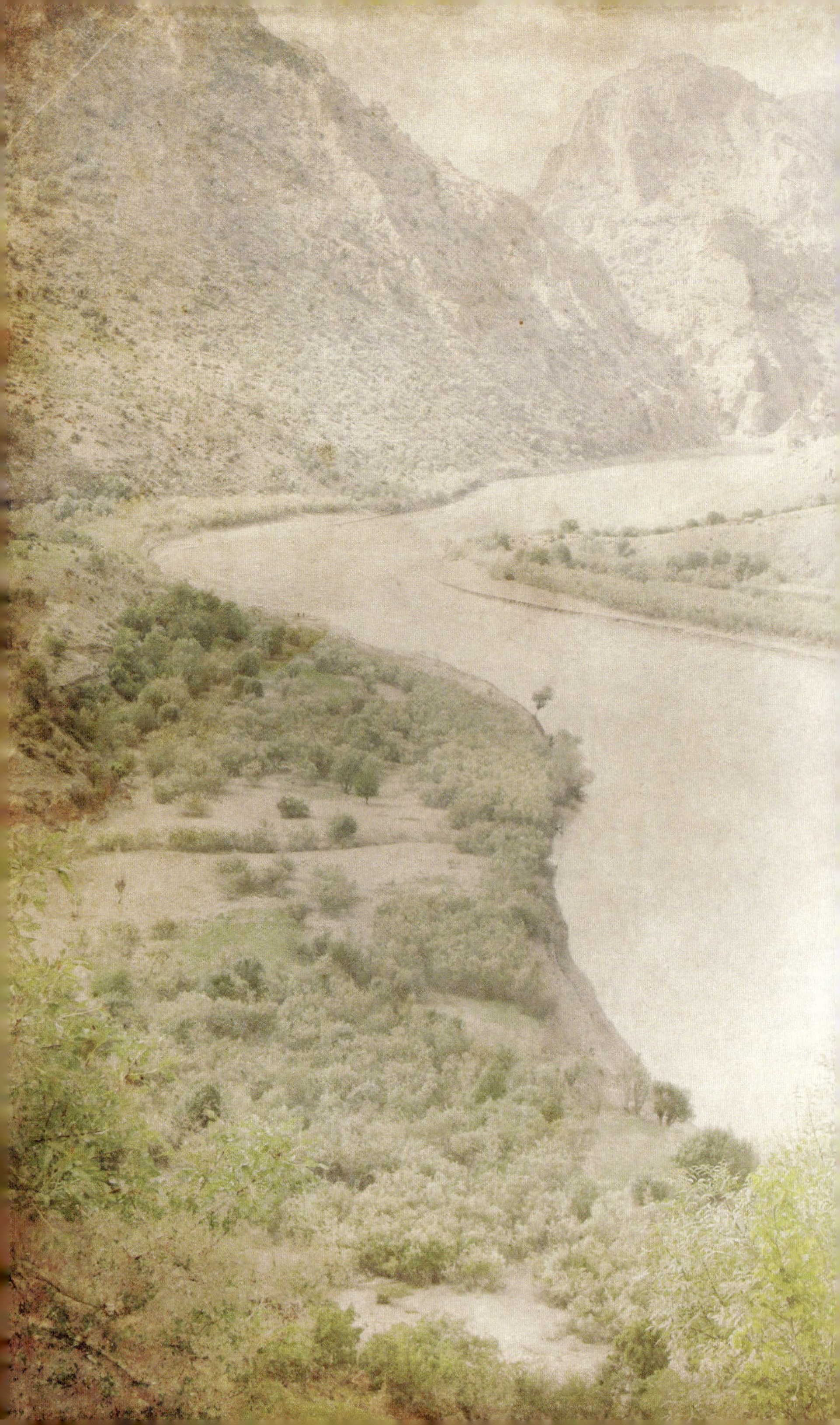

PART THREE

Works of Sorrow

Mt. Ararat

We experienced the physical adventures of driving through canyons and remote villages, but we also experienced emotional and spiritual adventures: adapting to a new culture, making new friends, and relying on God for direction.

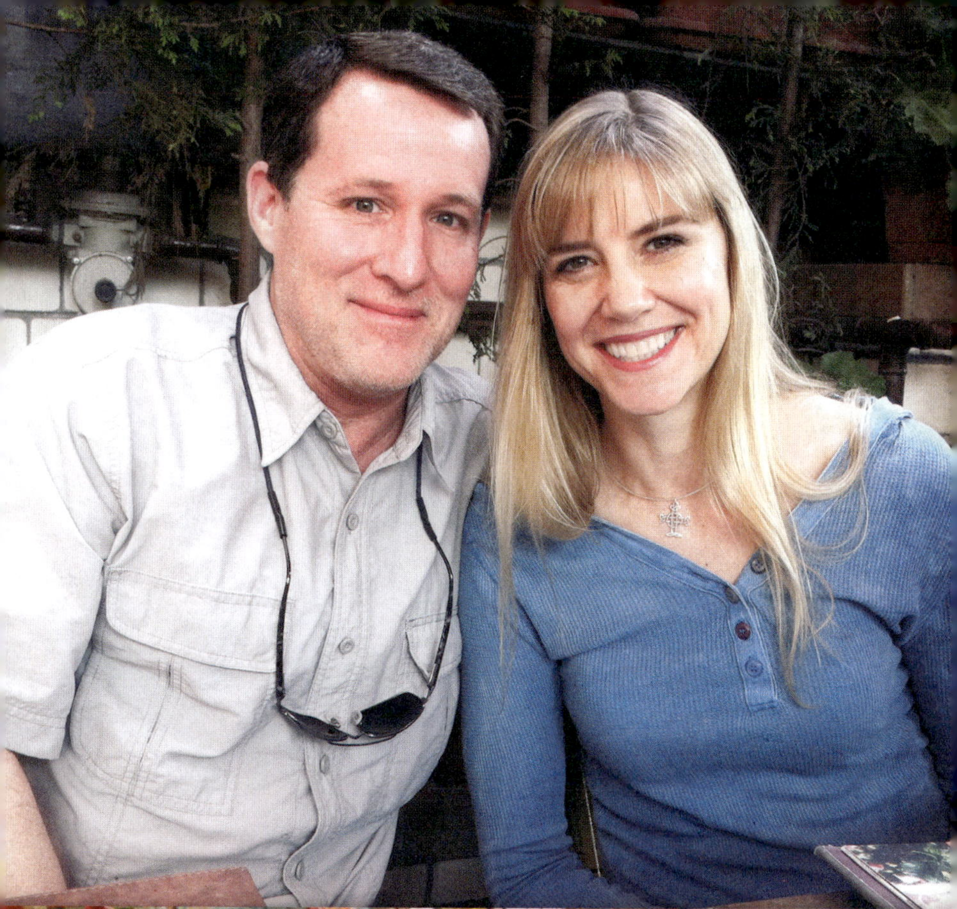

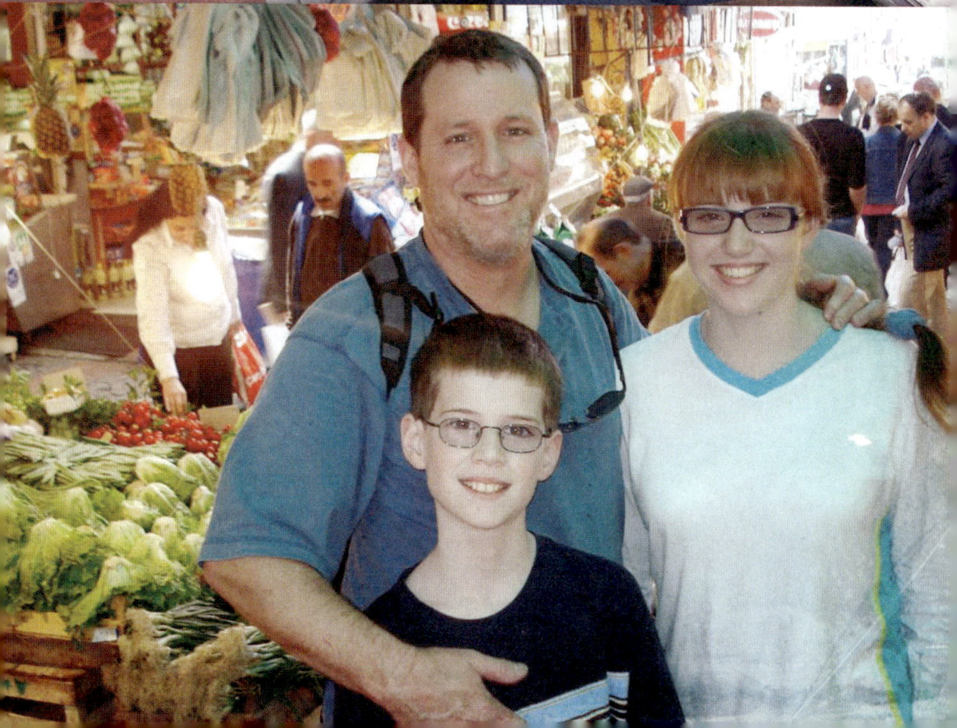

Journeys

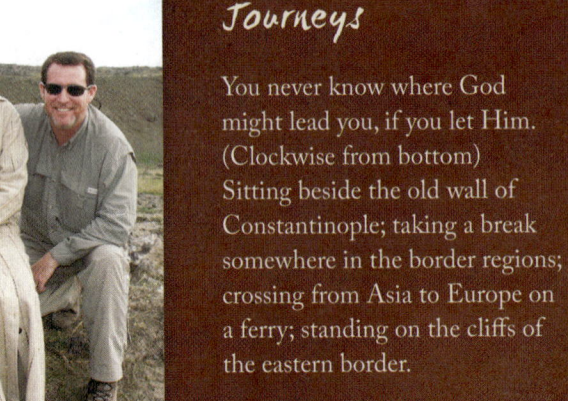

You never know where God might lead you, if you let Him. (Clockwise from bottom) Sitting beside the old wall of Constantinople; taking a break somewhere in the border regions; crossing from Asia to Europe on a ferry; standing on the cliffs of the eastern border.

XII. YÜZYIL İPEK YOLU
CENTURY SILK ROAD

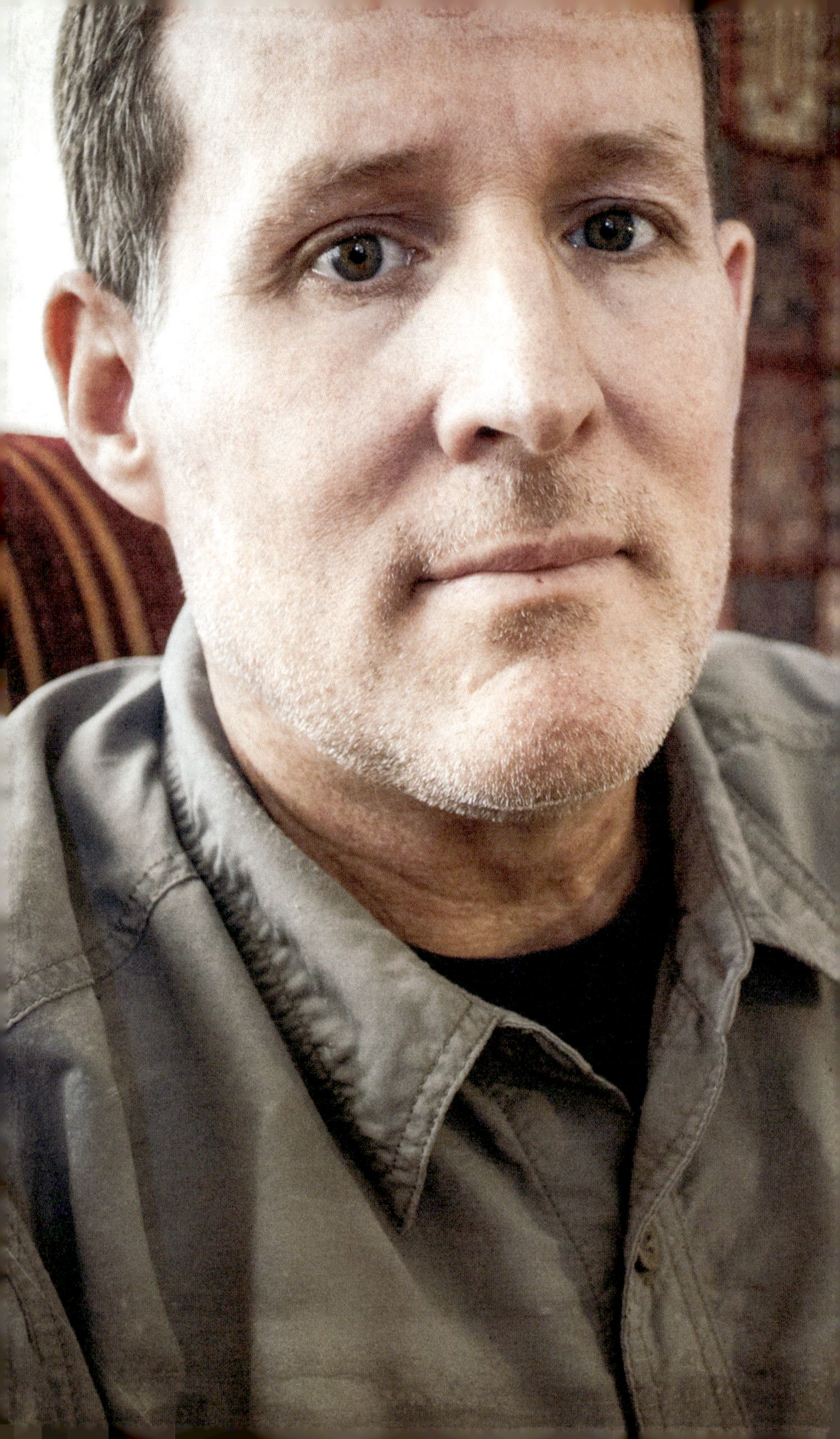

Works of Sorrow

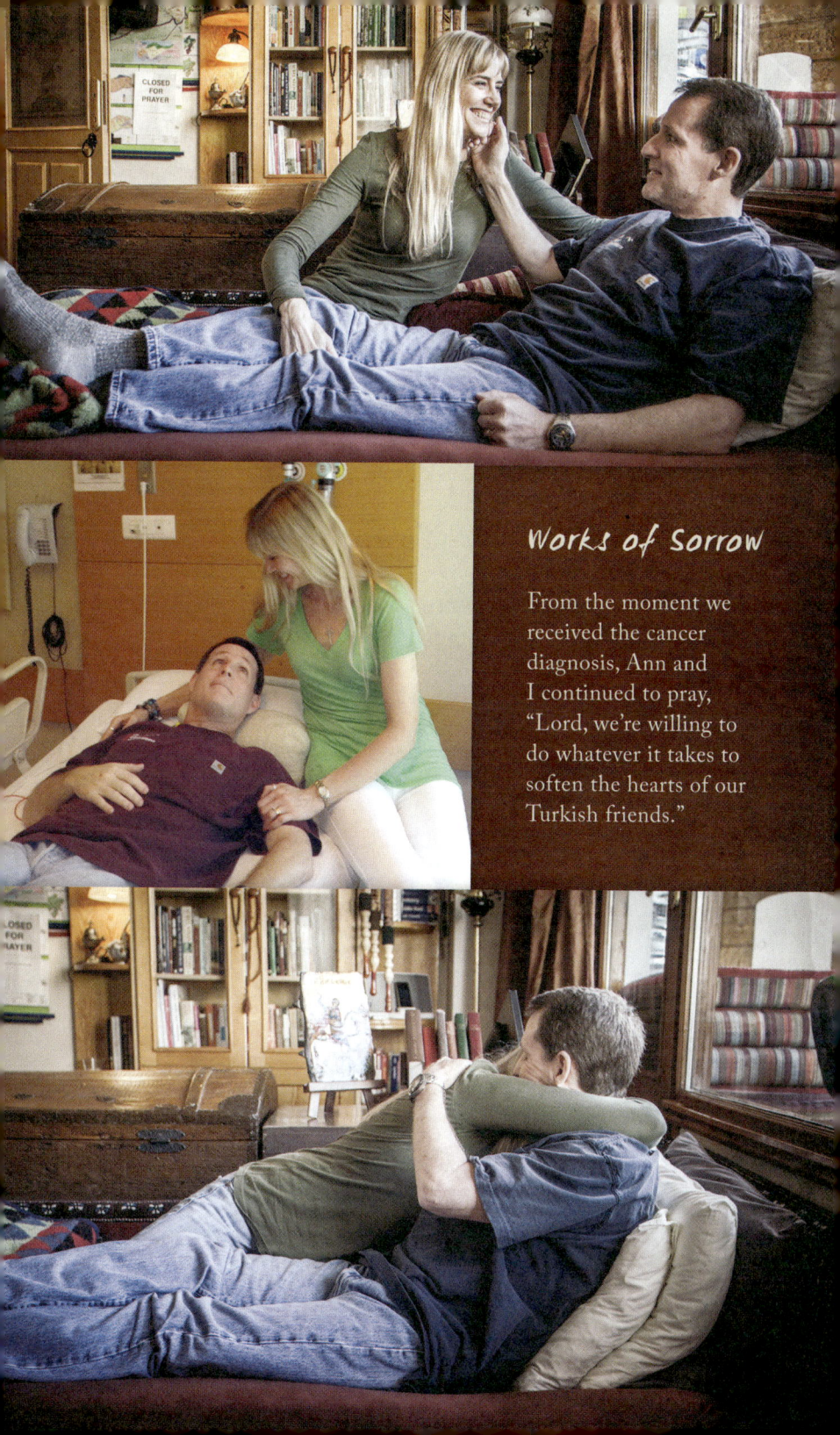

From the moment we received the cancer diagnosis, Ann and I continued to pray, "Lord, we're willing to do whatever it takes to soften the hearts of our Turkish friends."

"Our ultimate joy comes only from following Christ all the way to heaven."

— DALE AHLQUIST

CLOSED
FOR
PRAYER

Turkey
THE
CONCISE
OXFORD
DICTIONARY
OXFORD

We love the Turkish people.

CHAPTER 16
A SIXTH CALL TO PRAYER

*Those who sow with tears will reap with songs of joy.
Those who go out weeping, carrying seed to sow, will return
with songs of joy, carrying sheaves with them.*

PSALM 126:5

IF YOU WALK ALONG certain parts of the Bosporus Strait in the morning, you'll see empty fishing boats bobbing up and down in the choppy waves that dance against the piers. The narrow oars left by the fishermen clunk rhythmically against the insides of the boats, and barnacles grow on the brightly-painted, wooden hulls. The water is a deep navy blue—a color that makes it rather easy to believe that these swells, this moving, shifting current flows down from the Black Sea.

The Bosporus is a busy strait with huge freighters and oil tankers easing up the middle where the water is deepest. Two suspension bridges connect the Asian and European sides of Istanbul, their lanes constantly saturated with slow-moving traffic—if it's moving at all. Numerous ferries shuttle people back and forth from places like Üsküdar and Eminönü.

As the Bosporus gathers itself and makes one last turn before entering the Sea of Marmara (which leads into the Dardanelles, then the Aegean Sea, and finally the Mediterranean), it passes through the old city of Istanbul, what used to be known as Constantinople. For at least two thousand years this has been a strategic center for the entire region. Controlling the Bosporus now means controlling naval access to the Black Sea and the coasts of Bulgaria, Romania, Ukraine, Russia, and Georgia. Istanbul and the Bosporus Strait form one of the most strategic spots on the globe.

A few streets in from the banks of the Bosporus, in the web of villages that form Istanbul, you hear the men at their stands in the various bazaars, calling out in Turkish to the passersby.

"Come! Come look! You won't find prices like this anywhere else!"

"Now is the time to buy! Now is the time to buy!"

"Over here, ma'am! Over here is where the best prices are!"

Their voices echo through the streets.

They sell nuts and dried fruit, fresh produce and spices, clothing and accessories. The prices are competitive, and the majority of their customers are local. Their items are often stacked in fancy piles: pyramids of apples, squared-off blocks of curry spice, mounds of pecans. Everything is balanced precariously on the edge of collapse. If they see that you don't have a watch, they'll try to sell you one. If you don't carry an umbrella while it's raining, they'll gently steer you towards their umbrella stand.

"Sir, it's raining. Would you like to buy an umbrella? Only five *lira?*"

A SIXTH CALL TO PRAYER

When you stand along the Bosporus and look out over its steady movement, when you look out towards either bank, you'll see minarets pointing upwards throughout the city. Five times a day the call to prayer rises in a distinctive voice, scratched out through megaphone speakers attached to the top of the minarets. The muezzins range from local volunteers to national celebrities and their ancient sounding voices seem to come at you through a time machine.

Roughly translated, this is what they say in their calls to prayer:

Allah is great!
Allah is great!
Allah is great!
Allah is great!
I bear witness that there is no god except Allah.
I bear witness that there is no god except Allah.
I bear witness that Muhammad is the messenger of Allah.
I bear witness that Muhammad is the messenger of Allah.
Rise up for prayer.
Rise up for prayer.
Rise up for salvation.
Rise up for salvation.
Allah is great!
Allah is great!
There is no god except Allah.

During the pre-dawn prayer, when morning has yet to break over the city, when people are just beginning to stir in their houses, make their coffee, and start their cars for work, the following phrase is added after the fifth part:

> *Prayer is better than sleep.*
> *Prayer is better than sleep.*

These five daily calls to prayer form the basis of a Turkish day. There are few places you can go in Istanbul where the call will not reach you. When you wake in the morning, you hear the muezzin calling everyone to prayer. Throughout the day, you are reminded to pray. When darkness falls, once again you hear another call to prayer.

Most of the people living in Istanbul do not attend all five prayers. This is a secular city pulled between the influence of Europe and the traditions of the Middle East, and most practicing Muslims only go to the main service held on Fridays. Yet the call to prayer forms a constant backdrop to life in the city, something you can't ignore.

* * * * * *

Somewhere on the Asian side of Istanbul, not far from where the Bosporus flows into the Sea of Marmara and only a few miles from one of the ferry ports that shuttle people from one continent to the other, an imam walks down the cobblestone sidewalks. His day is consumed by the mosque. He leads prayers there five times a day for thirty to forty-five minutes each session. His family lives in the adjoining house. With any extra time he can find, he performs administrative duties pertaining to the mosque.

In addition to that, he spends a lot of time walking the streets, connecting with those under his care. The men greet him, not with the typical Turkish word for hello but with the more religious, *"salaam alaikum,"* or "peace to you." He knows they act a little differently when he's around. He hopes his presence brings peace to the community.

> "All we have to decide is what to do with the time that is given us."
> -J. R. R. Tolkien, *The Lord of the Rings: The Fellowship of the Ring*

But on this day, he's distracted. He isn't thinking about the next call to prayer or the paperwork sitting on his desk. He isn't thinking about the people walking the streets or about his three children. Something else is on his mind; he thoughtfully considers the news he heard earlier in the day regarding his Christian friend, Stan Steward.

He turns over the prayer beads in his pocket: thirty-three beads. Reciting the ninety-nine names of Allah, he cycles through them three times. The small, round beads are smooth and familiar. He thinks of how Stan and his family have become an integral part of their community. He reaches up and adjusts his glasses.

Then he decides. *Yes, I will do it!*

Later, at the cell-phone shop, the men sit and talk politics and soccer and business. The call to prayer sounds, and the older men rise slowly and walk down the street to the mosque.

Meanwhile, those remaining in the shop continue talking.

"Have you heard?" one of the men asks.

"Heard what?"

"About the sixth call to prayer?"

"No! A sixth call to prayer?"

"Yes!" he says. "The imam will issue a sixth call to prayer for Stan Steward."

A sixth call to prayer! This is done only for very special, very devout men! But the men in the cell-phone shop aren't surprised. They nod their heads quietly, and one gets up and walks quickly out of the shop. He's a special friend of this man, Stan Steward, and to cry in front of the other men would be shameful.

… A SIXTH CALL TO PRAYER

*Ann and I are
co-adventurers
for Christ.*

CHAPTER 17
PREPARED FOR LOSS

"Abide in me."
JOHN 15:4 KJV

THE WORD GOD GAVE me echoed over and over in my mind: *Sometimes works of sorrow, loss, and sacrifice speak louder than signs, wonders, and miracles.*

It was a heavy word to receive. The message was unmistakable. There would be a cost . . . a sacrifice . . . something we'd have to give to reach the people of Turkey. I realized that our small corner of this country wasn't going to be changed by signs and wonders. It would be changed only by sorrow and sacrifice.

God began preparing us for loss.

* * * * * *

Our Silk Road Expeditions, when we would head out for weeks at a time into the undeveloped areas of central Turkey, were tough. They weren't just travel adventures. Of course they were amazing and the sights we saw were incredible. The culture and the villages and the history we encountered were unlike anything we'd ever seen before. But each one of the twenty or so trips we'd been on had been fraught with obstacles and danger and discomfort.

Leading up to those trips, we always encountered illnesses, financial challenges, and spiritual struggles. There was rarely enough money to do it right, never enough equipment. Often the equipment we did have was on its last leg, and we didn't have any backup. A two-week trip cost about $2,000 once we paid for gas, food, and lodging. Every time we left on one of our expeditions, it was always with a huge amount of faith that God was going to supply what we needed.

Then came the trip planned for the fall of 2012. During the lead-up to that SRE, we felt the excitement rising. God had focused our hearts on a particular area—about 100 square miles of Turkey centered in the Dark Canyon. We didn't know of any other missionaries working there. Maybe someone was out there, but we never crossed paths with them. For us it was uncharted territory.

I felt an unusual heaviness going into that trip. Elle had just left for college, and I think Ann and I were both dealing with the fact that within a year Stanley would go as well, leaving just the two of us at home. Many parents look forward to the day their kids leave home and embark on their own journeys. But this wasn't how Ann and I felt. It was a difficult thing for us to process, this idea that our tight family unit would be dispersed around the globe. We knew it was necessary and important for Elle and Stanley, and we looked forward to a new stage in our own relationship, but it would take some getting used to.

Apart from Elle's recent departure, there was also this sense that the expedition we were about to embark on was a crucial one . . . monumental. Ann and I had a sense that what would happen on that trip would change everything.

The day before we left, Ann prayed about some of these things.

God, we've yet to see some movement toward salvation. We've been here in Turkey for seven years, we've prayed and we've seen miracles. We've poured our lives into this community as well as the villages we've run across on our SREs. But no one is being saved.

We've seen Your amazing favor. We've felt Your protection. We've been in areas where we've had to get through military checkpoints and You've brought us through. We've been on roads we had no earthly business traveling on. We've heard of car bombs and terrorist attacks happening soon after we left a place, and we've watched as the military cleared the roads of mines around and in front of us.

> "The question that God asked Ann is such an important one for this generation: 'Are you willing to suffer?' The truth is, all of us will suffer, whether or not we're willing. If we approach suffering with an unwilling heart, if we fight against it and seek to avoid it at all cost, it can destroy us. But if we're willing to suffer, if we're open to what God can accomplish through our suffering, then our joy and hope will be evident to everyone around us."
>
> —Stan

> "I am the LORD your God, who teaches you what is best for you, who directs you in the way you should go."
> —Isaiah 48:17

You've always been with us. And we've seen amazing things.

But what is it going to take to change the hearts of our Muslim friends?

We'll do anything, God! We counted the cost before we ever came to Turkey. We wanted to go where no one was going. We knew we were going into a country where any of us could lose our lives in a moment.

We've never looked for safety, God, only for You to use us. I've put my kids in Your hands, and I know they are Yours. I'm willing for You to do whatever it takes.

Can we see one person saved? Can we see one person decide to follow You?

Whatever the cost, God. We lay down our own hopes and dreams.

Then she felt that God asked her a question: *Are you willing to suffer?*

She felt like she had answered that question so many times. Throughout the years, it seemed like God had repeatedly said to us, *If you'll trust Me, if you'll follow Me, there's more.* Both Ann and I felt like we had decided so many times to walk the way of trust. We understood that suffering would sometimes be part of that path. So when God asked Ann if she was willing to suffer, she felt much like Peter when God questioned his commitment three times.

God, Ann replied, *I thought we'd settled this a long time ago. I'm willing to suffer . . . no matter the cost.*

As Ann continued to pray, she had a vision of her right hand bleeding profusely. She marveled at the sheer amount of blood coming from her hand. Questions crept into her mind.

God, she asked, *what does this mean? Am I going to be crippled?*

God gave an answer: *If you will abide in Me, this will not cripple you.*

Ann's response again was, *God, whatever it takes. Your will be done . . . whatever the cost.*

Then a thought entered her mind. She continued to see the vision of her bloodied hand . . . and suddenly she had a moment of clarity.

Stan is my right hand. God, is this a vision of what will happen to Stan?

But God didn't give Ann a yes or a no. Not at that point. God simply came back with the same answer He had given her before: *If you will abide in Me, this will not cripple you.*

She closed her journal quietly. Elle had left for college only a few days before, and Ann wondered if this vision, this premonition, was a result of all the emotions she felt regarding her daughter traveling alone to the States. Our family was changing. It wasn't an easy time.

Ann decided not to tell anyone about the vision right away—not even me. She went on with the normal routine of her day, but the exchange with God echoed in her mind.

Stan is my right hand. God, is this Stan? . . . If you abide in Me, this will not cripple you.

*Stanley and I
wait for a train.*

Scan this code to watch a video
introduction to this chapter.

CHAPTER 18
PREMONITIONS AND SIGNS

*May the righteous be glad and rejoice before God;
may they be happy and joyful.*

PSALM 68:3

WE FINISHED OUR FINAL packing for the upcoming expedition with plans to leave the next day. Ann hadn't yet shared with me her vision. If I thought she seemed a little quiet, I chalked it up to Elle having left for college just days before. There's a lot to do to prepare for one of these expeditions, so between packing the truck, checking our equipment, and praying over road maps the evening passed quickly.

You should probably know that for several weeks and months leading up to that trip, I'd been experiencing some strange physical symptoms. Nothing too severe, but I noticed that my stamina seemed to be decreasing, even though Ann and I would walk five miles together each day. I'd also had some minor abdominal pain. Strangest of all, I was losing weight . . . but I chalked that up to exercise and eating right, and to be honest I felt pretty good about the number on the scale.

Late that night, as we continued preparing for the trip, I got a message from a good friend of mine who lived in San Diego. He was a detective with the San Diego Police Department—a tough, practical guy who certainly hasn't gotten as far as he has by making overly emotional decisions. That's why his message gave us reason to pause.

"Listen, I'm not a person who sees visions," he told me. "But I was walking out to my car and became overwhelmed with thoughts of your family . . . thoughts that your family might be under attack in Turkey. I'll be honest—I was so overwhelmed that it scared me. I didn't even know if I should let you know, that's how afraid I was, and I didn't want to disturb you needlessly. But I talked to my pastor, and he said I should tell you."

I told Ann about the message. By now it was getting fairly late on the night before we planned to leave.

Ann waited until I finished . . . then sighed.

"Okay," she said. "Maybe you should read my journal."

We sat down, and I read through the vision of her bloody right hand. She explained the details of it to me. We speculated on what it might mean.

"It seems to me that if we go on this SRE, there's a very real chance of us being attacked," I said. We talked openly about that possibility. Would we be killed by terrorists on a dirt road in central Turkey? Would we lose Stanley? Would we all be killed by a roadside bomb or a landmine? Would we be kidnapped and held for ransom or executed? None of these were new scenarios. All were things we'd considered prior to any other SRE, but we did want to be wise. We decided to pray and sleep on it until morning.

In the morning I contacted our country's mission leader within our denomination and asked him if this was something we should spread the word about. We wanted as much prayer support as possible but didn't want to alarm people unnecessarily. That's when he told us of something that had happened at a prayer meeting he'd attended the night before.

In a vision, a woman saw a glass canopy over Turkey and it was suffocating the people. There was no air, no life, and the entire country was dry and barren because of that glass dome. Everything was dying. But then she saw a hand thrust up through the canopy, shattering the glass.

> Blessed is the one who perseveres under trial because, having stood the test, that person will receive the crown of life that the Lord has promised to those who love him.
>
> —James 1:12

The hand that broke the dome was wounded and bloody.

As Ann and I thought of that description a solemn feeling descended on us.

"In breaking the glass, the hand brought air and water and a chance for the Turkish people to live. But there was a cost of blood that went along with it."

Once again I was reminded of our pleas with God all these years: *Bring life to our Turkish friends, God . . . no matter the cost.*

And I remembered His recent words to me: *Sometimes works of sorrow, loss, and sacrifice speak louder than signs, wonders, and miracles.*

So this was the cost.

After we got off the phone with our mission leader, we pondered the many different scenarios. Whatever it was that we were going to face, it seemed that it would be a sacrifice worth making. We were willing to do anything if it meant bringing life to Turkey. Again, as He had so many times before, God seemed to be asking us if we were willing. We knew what our decision was. We'd always done whatever God asked us to do, and that wasn't going to change now.

Driving out of the city the next morning, leaving Istanbul behind and rumbling out onto the rough country roads, we were surrounded by a supernatural peace. In the back of our minds, both Ann and I thought that the impending sacrifice would be a roadside bomb. We'd seen the effects of so many mines and bombs during our previous SREs, so it didn't seem out of the question.

Also, just a few days before we left, a local politician had been kidnapped from the part of Turkey where we were going. They were still looking for him when we left Istanbul. There had been many kidnappings in that region of unrest, so that also seemed a possibility.

But as the trip progressed, we were amazed. We found unmarked dirt roads that led us deep into the mountains. Everywhere we stopped, people begged us to stay with them or go hunting with them or eat with them. We had the opportunity to pray with people over and over again. For the first time in Turkey, we weren't looking for ways to convince the villagers to accept us—they were pursuing us!

God brought Ann's attention to Psalm 68:

May God arise, may his enemies be scattered;
may his foes flee before him.
May you blow them away like smoke—
as wax melts before the fire,
may the wicked perish before God.
But may the righteous be glad
and rejoice before God;
may they be happy and joyful.
Sing to God, sing in praise of his name,
extol him who rides on the clouds;
*rejoice before him—his name is the L*ORD.
A father to the fatherless, a defender of widows,
is God in his holy dwelling.
God sets the lonely in families,
he leads out the prisoners with singing;
but the rebellious live in a sun-scorched land.

It felt like our enemies had been scattered and new ways were opening up to us. Seemingly, every corner we turned revealed, not a roaming group of terrorists as we had expected but a nomadic tribe just waiting for us to visit with them and pray over them. We found ourselves rejoicing during the entire trip.

God gave us such incredible favor. One particular event stands out—a visit to a village where we'd been before. We always prayed with our village friends before we left, but this time they had some other family members with them and I wasn't sure what to do. Would it be strange for their relatives if we prayed for them? Would they appreciate our prayers, or would they be resistant to our Christian presence?

> "Anything worth something has a cost. In the same way that precious things cannot be bought without large sums of money, important transitions cannot happen unless someone pays a price. Luke 14:28 says, 'Suppose one of you wants to build a tower. Won't you first sit down and estimate the cost to see if you have enough money to complete it?' What would you like to see happen in the lives of those around you? Have you counted the cost?"
>
> -Stan

The situation became even more uncomfortable when the time came to say good-bye and we were out on the street, surrounded by a lot of people milling around. It's one thing to pray for people in the privacy of their own home, but it's another thing to pray for them on the sidewalk in the middle of a Turkish village where everyone practices a traditional form of Islam. Yet we were determined not to miss this opportunity, so we prayed.

I told them I would pray for our friend's husband, that he would find a job, and then I started praying in the Spirit. I wasn't sure how they would respond, but when I opened my eyes, everyone was weeping. The Spirit had come down and moved in that little prayer circle. Our friend's sister grabbed Ann's hand and said with determined sincerity, "I understood that inside!"

The next day her husband got a job.

At another point on the trip we came upon a nomadic tribe whose portable village was just off the road. I parked the truck and walked towards them, and they immediately greeted us and insisted that we stay for dinner. Stanley and I took off our sandals and sat in the shade of a large tree on a small blanket where one of the shepherds was sitting. Behind us, one of their small canvas tents was staked into the tan-colored earth with long sticks. Off in the distance, a rectangular mud hut sat perched on the hillside, and a wash line hung from one of its corners, connected to a nearby tree.

I asked the men about their animals and their lives as nomads. Another man came out and sat down with his back to the tree. I wondered if he'd dressed up just for us: he wore a Scottish cap, black dress pants and shoes, a light-blue collared shirt, and a black suit coat. His face was weathered, and his bushy white eyebrows protruded up over his sunglasses.

He perched a clarinet-like instrument in his mouth, just below his broad, white moustache, and played this beautiful, whimsical music. The man beside us on the blanket played a large, round drum of animal hide. There Stanley and I sat, on a hillside in central Turkey, spending time with these lovely nomadic people. I looked over to the other side of the tree, and there was Ann, dancing with some of the village women, her long tunic flowing around her. I smiled . . . how I loved that woman.

That afternoon they offered us their water and bread, and they killed a goat so we could have a feast. I prayed with them before we left, and Ann, Stanley, and I continued to marvel at how God's favor had been so obviously bestowed on our trip.

* * * * * *

During the drive back to Istanbul, near the end of the trip, I started feeling pain under my rib cage. It started as a dull ache then peaked to the point where I could barely handle it. I moved around in the driver's seat, trying to find a comfortable position. I stopped the truck more often than usual so I could get out and walk around. Nothing seemed to ease the discomfort.

"Wow, this is killing me," I told Ann. "I think you're going to have to drive."

She looked at me with a strange expression. I couldn't remember the last time that we'd traveled together and she had driven. It was just one of those unspoken things in our marriage: I always drove.

"Are you going to be okay?" she asked as I pulled to the side and we switched seats.

"Yeah," I said, trying to stretch out in the passenger seat. "That food was pretty greasy last night. It's either that or I picked up a nasty bug from drinking the water. I might have to go back on antibiotics when we get home."

Just the thought of that medication made me groan. I'd taken it the year before in an attempt to get rid of a particularly nasty bug I'd picked up somewhere, and that medication just about killed me. It's an extremely powerful antibiotic, and my body had done its best to reject it. I hoped that what I was experiencing was just a severe case of indigestion . . . but I had my doubts.

So Ann drove the rest of the way home, and I tried to think about anything besides the terrible pain in my side. We drove mile after mile, first on winding, dirt roads, then on stones, which slowly became paved roads. Finally we pulled onto the highway . . . soon we'd be in Istanbul.

Even with that terrible ache in my abdomen, I had to smile as we entered the city. What was all that stuff about danger?

PREMONITIONS AND SIGNS

What had been the deal with all those premonitions and signs? It was the best SRE we'd ever gone on! Ann and I talked about Psalm 68 again, especially the middle part where it talks about the righteous being glad and rejoicing. That was us—we were thrilled how God had used us on that journey, and we couldn't wait to return home, get plugged back in with our Turkish family, and plan our next SRE.

As soon as we got back, I made an appointment with the doctor to get my abdominal issues sorted out. I had no idea that all of the puzzle pieces were about to come together.

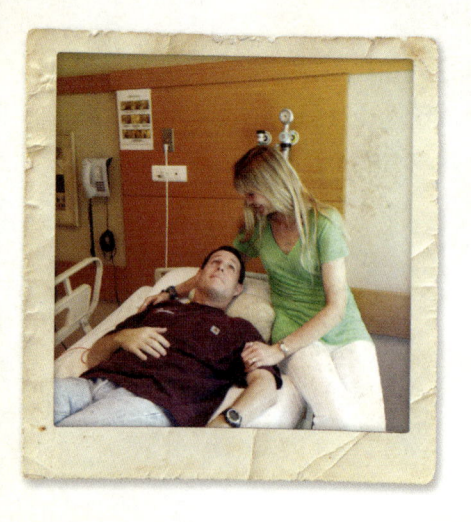

Ann and I in the hospital shortly after my diagnosis.

Scan this code to watch a video
introduction to this chapter.

CHAPTER 19
THE DOCTOR'S DIAGNOSIS

I will sing to the LORD all my life; I will sing praise to my God as long as I live. May my meditation be pleasing to him, as I rejoice in the LORD.

PSALM 104:33

BY THE TIME we arrived in Istanbul, the pain in my abdomen was sharp and deep. Home from our expedition, I spent the first day in bed, hoping that it was something rest could cure. But it didn't subside, so Ann and I went to the doctor to be tested.

We both figured it was giardia, a water-born parasite you can get from drinking contaminated water. Once it gets into your intestines it multiplies quickly, just sort of takes over, and it does a real number on your body. It's microscopic, and I thought I'd also had it a few years prior. The antibiotic for giardia is one of the strongest around, and it can lay you flat for about ten days, so I didn't want to take it unless they were absolutely sure that's what I had.

The doctor was fairly certain that was my problem, so he put me on antibiotics on August 29. I went back to see him again eight days later.

"I feel worse," I told him. "This thing just isn't giving up. Shouldn't I feel better by now?"

"Continue taking the medication," he said, but he was also perplexed as to why I wasn't feeling any better, so he immediately started doing various other tests.

"If it's up under your ribs, it could be pneumonia," he said. He listened carefully to my lungs. I tried to breathe normally.

"Hmmm," he said. "It sounds a bit off. I think it might be pneumonia."

He wrote out an order for an x-ray. In Turkey, you pay for everything separately as you receive the service. So we took his note down to the x-ray technician. He took several films and gave us the developed images. We paid him, and then we went back up to the doctor.

I had glanced at the x-rays on the way back up to the doctor's office, and by the time we got up there I thought I knew the diagnosis.

I pointed at a few small light areas in the image and wondered if that might be pneumonia as the doctor had suspected.

"See there?" I asked Ann. "Besides, I've had pneumonia in the past. It's something I have to watch out for."

Ann looked at me and shrugged, and in that moment we were relieved. Pneumonia—that must be my problem. I tried to think back through what the treatment might be, and how long it would take for me to recover. The holidays were right around the corner and, besides, I wanted to get back out and see my friends in the community.

The doctor studied the images for a few moments, but his diagnosis differed from mine.

"No," he said, sighing and looking up at me. "This isn't pneumonia. Those light areas are simply scar tissue, perhaps from the last time you had pneumonia. I'm going to send you down for an ultrasound of your abdomen."

Ann and I walked back downstairs.

> "It's so easy for the things that cause us sorrow to take root in our hearts as bitterness or despair. But our sorrows, and how we handle them, can be just as powerful a tool for the kingdom as victories or miracles—perhaps even more so. Don't squander your sorrows."
>
> —Stan

This is kind of ridiculous, I thought, *all of this fuss for nothing.*

I stretched out on the table, and the technician put a cold gel on my stomach and scanned my abdomen. We were there for a few minutes, and his face didn't change expression the entire time. Later I would think back on that and realize that he must be extremely good at his job, considering he was able to keep a straight face while looking at such terrible images.

"You need to go downstairs and get an MRI," he said without any explanation.

I shrugged. Why not? I was doing everything else. I might as well get an MRI while I was at it. So Ann and I went downstairs for the MRI. While we waited for the results, my doctor checked me into the emergency room and a nurse put an IV in my arm.

What's going on around here? It's not that big of a deal.

> "Isaiah 55:6-7 says we should 'Seek the LORD while he may be found; call on him while he is near. Let the wicked forsake their ways and the unrighteous their thoughts. Let them turn to the LORD, and he will have mercy on them, and to our God, for he will freely pardon.' If we can somehow help those around us find Him, they will find mercy. This is my job. This is our job."
>
> —Stan

I looked at Ann.

"I give them three hours and then I'm out of here," I said.

I even took a photo of the IV and uploaded it to my Facebook page, captioning it with one word: "Balderdash."

We were in the emergency room looking through a glass window into another room where the doctor sat at a desk. Then the MRI imagery came back. He sat at his desk and stared at the images. Then he got up and paced into the other room, as if he'd forgotten something. He looked flustered. Then he sat down at the computer and looked at MRI images again. Then he got up and paced some more.

"Come over here and look at this," he finally said. By now he was extremely agitated.

The nurse unhooked the IV and we went behind the desk and watched the MRI film pan through the images of my liver. Each image was a picture of a thin slice of my liver, and there were white spots from one end of each image to the other. It was like looking at a constellation of stars zoomed in real close. Black was good and white was bad. The pictures were covered in white.

"Is this normal?" Ann asked hesitantly pointing to a large white cluster.

He cried out as if he were in pain.

"No, it's bad! It's very bad! That area is dying."

We both felt terrible for the doctor. He was so affected by the images. He kept saying, *"Bak! Bak! Bak!"* (Look! Look! Look!) as he went through the images. He normally spoke to us in English, but due to the shock of the images he was speaking Turkish. His distress was palpable. I thought he might start weeping.

My liver was full of uncountable lesions. There was also a conglomerate, an interconnecting web of cancer. A realization washed over me—this was it . . . this was how we were going to break down the wall of Islam. This would be my work of sorrow.

The doctor put his head in his hands and shook it back and forth.

"Is it cancer?" I asked, but I already knew the answer.

"Yes," he said quietly. "Yes."

In that moment, God gave me the feeling that my death would help to lead my Turkish Muslim friends to Him. I don't think God gives people cancer; I'm not saying He made me sick. But in that moment, God was saying something to Ann and to me: *This is the path. This is the right road. This is of Me. You are okay—this is My plan. Trust Me.*

"Wait," the doctor said. "Maybe it's not cancer. Maybe it's something else. We should do more tests."

I looked in the doctor's eyes, made sure he was listening, and said, "I know it's cancer."

When the doctor walked out, Ann and I looked at each other.

"Cancer," I said.

It was like the veil had lifted. We understood the plan. We recognized in that moment how everything was coming together. This disease, this sorrow, this cancer—for so many years we'd prayed for something that would shake our Turkish community, something that would open their hearts.

In that moment, I felt oceans of grace.

A gentle and generous Turk who befriended me on an SRE through central Turkey.

CHAPTER 20
WHATEVER THE COST

All die. Those who die for Christ should be considered neither heroic nor foolish. Dying is a normal part of the Christian life. We have one life to live and one death to die.

DICK BROGDEN

WE WAITED A FEW DAYS before sharing the news with our Turkish community because we knew they would take it hard. We hated to introduce them to this pain, but we prayed that God would use the coming storm of sorrow to break down the walls that kept them from Jesus. But even with that hope, it was still difficult to deliver news like that to people we loved.

Ann told her Turkish sister first, and she wept. She couldn't believe it. But more than that, she was so sad that they'd been away when we first found out.

"I'm so sorry you had to do this alone," she told Ann.

Ann's Turkish sister had lost her brother when he was relatively young, and we knew she would take the news hard because she saw me as her brother.

"It's serious. It's in a very late stage. And we don't know how to tell Mom," Ann said, referring to her Turkish mother.

"Okay. Then we'll tell her together."

So our Turkish sister called in our mom and, along with Ann, they talked about the weather and other light-hearted things. Then Ann asked her to sit down.

"We have some news. Stan's been sick while you were gone, and we've been to the doctor."

Our Turkish mother took it very hard at first before quickly moving into denial.

"Maybe it's just a stomach bug!" she proclaimed.

"No," our Turkish sister told her in a matter-of-fact voice. "It's serious."

In the days and weeks to follow, our Turkish mother would come to our house and sit on a green stool and stare vacantly out the window. She cried quietly during those times, lonely tears that left narrow trails running down her cheeks. She wanted to be with us, she wanted to support us with her presence, but she also didn't want to cry in front of me. So she looked out the window and watched as the seagulls floated among the buildings and the gray winter sky dropped down, just above where we sat.

It was hard to see the devastating emotions my diagnosis brought to our friends.

* * * * * *

There's a culturally correct way to deliver difficult news in Turkey. In America, we tend to believe it's best to rip off the Band-Aid quickly, get it over with, but in Turkey you introduce bad news in stages. You might take a week to deliver it in various steps. Perhaps you first tell your friends about the signs and symptoms, the pain you're having, and the questions you have. Then a day or two later you might tell them you have scheduled a doctor's appointment. A few days after that you might mention that things don't look good. Then, finally, perhaps a week down the road, you tell them the full diagnosis.

But we didn't realize this right away, and Ann told one of our friends in the Dark Canyon village a little too suddenly. This woman is such a dear friend and she lives far away so Ann didn't feel there was any reason not to share the news with her over the phone.

"We took Stan to the doctor," Ann said, "because he's been very sick. Now the doctor has told us he has cancer."

At that point, Ann heard grief-stricken shouting from the other end of the phone line.

"Hayırdır! Hayırdır!" ("No! No!")

Ann knew she'd broken the news too quickly, but there was no turning back at that point, so she just kept moving forward with added details.

"Yes. It's been found late . . . there's no possibility of surgery . . ." she paused, then continued, "and he doesn't have long to live."

Ann's friend started sobbing hysterically. Ann didn't know what to do, so she asked if the friend's neighbor was home. The woman needed someone to be with her.

The next day Ann called her again, and she started crying right away, but Ann was able to pray with her. The next time they spoke on the phone, Ann's friend shared something that moved us deeply.

"My husband went to the mosque to pray for Stan. My family, my sister and her husband, everyone is praying for Stan."

Ann sent her a text message containing an encouraging scripture, how God would comfort her the way God comforts a child. Ann didn't call because she didn't want to upset her friend. But immediately the phone rang.

"I am nothing!" Ann's friend said. "Don't even think of me right now! Think only of Stan!"

We had to convince our Turkish friends that despite challenging circumstances, life continued . . . and we were at peace. We put all our energy into comforting them, trying to help them see how our faith gives us strength. I hope that through this process they've seen our unwavering faith. I hope they've seen Jesus.

God, I prayed, *our friends are going to the mosques to pray for me. They're taking this heavy burden and looking for answers. Meet them there! They're calling out to You on my behalf—show them Jesus!*

* * * * * *

Our doctor sent me to a cancer hospital where they performed a colonoscopy and discovered that the cancer had started in my colon before metastasizing to my liver. They confirmed the diagnosis: stage four colon cancer.

From the first moment I received the diagnosis in Istanbul, so many things made sense. The pain I'd felt in my stomach the year before hadn't been a bacterial infection at all; it had been the early phases of this disease. The nudging from God to pray differently—and the courage He gave us to submit our lives completely to Him—in the instant the doctor showed us the MRI images, we understood. It was like God was saying, *We have talked about this. I have asked you several times throughout the years if you are willing, and you have always said yes.*

It's not that God asked me to have cancer. It's that we asked God, "What will it take to bring our Muslim friends to Christ?" and this was the answer. This is what it will take. All along we've said, "Yes, God, we're willing . . . *whatever* the cost."

But in another way the diagnosis did take us by surprise because we thought the cost, the loss and destruction, would come from a rocket-propelled grenade aimed at the truck or a kidnapping. We thought the loss would come in a blaze of lights and fire. But we're so thankful that didn't happen, because if our family had suffered from an act of terrorism, people would've had one more reason to say how awful "those Muslims" are. Instead, through my struggle with cancer, our American friends see the sincere love poured out to us from our Turkish community. They hear about the villagers who call daily for updates, who weep for us, who offer to do anything

"I know some people want to ask, 'Where's your faith? Don't you think God can heal you? Why are you already planning the funeral?' Hopefully this story helps them to see why we're offering our sorrow to God as a willing sacrifice. We've seen miracles here, and they've had no visible effect on our community. We know God can heal, but we've always said we want to remain in the center of His will so He can use us to bring Muslims to Jesus."

—Stan

they can. We want our American friends to see the loveliness of Muslim people.

During those first few days after the diagnosis we still felt a sense of shock, but those were also the best days because there was so much grace in those moments. I could feel God's hand leading us along a peaceful way.

We've reasoned together, God said. *You agreed to do anything that was necessary. This is what's necessary, and I will be with you.*

So that's why, when people ask us how to pray, we say, "Pray for Muslims. Don't pray for my healing without first praying that God would save Muslims. We don't want my healing to happen at the expense of souls."

I believe that if God healed me right now, even such a miraculous sign wouldn't change our community. They've seen healings, and those signs and wonders did not result in people seeking Christ. Yet they see me now and their hearts are deeply affected. They see a man, a friend, dying of cancer, and that man still has hope. He still has joy. And they don't understand how that's possible.

> *Great peace have those who love your law, and nothing can make them stumble.*
> —Psalm 119:165

"Aren't you afraid of death?" my friend asks me, in one of those rare moments when he can keep his composure long enough to talk about my cancer. "Aren't you afraid to talk about death?"

"I'm not afraid," I say. "I know where I'm going, and I know Whom I'll be with. I know that Christ has prepared a home for me."

And because I'm sick, they don't argue. So I have a brand new doorway open in front of me where I can be bold and talk even more clearly about Jesus.

✶ ✶ ✶ ✶ ✶ ✶

When we returned from that last expedition, Ann felt like God was giving her Psalm 68 again. She thought she understood why that chapter stood out in her mind. Our trip had been such a huge success: our enemies had parted before us, and new ways had been opened. But the entire revelation didn't come to her until we were on our way out of the hospital, the cancer diagnosis fresh in our minds, because Psalm 68:5 says this:

> *A father to the fatherless, a defender of widows,*
> *is God in his holy dwelling.*
> *God sets the lonely in families. . . .*

"A father to the fatherless, a defender of widows . . . God sets the lonely in families. . . ." She realized that she was the widow in the psalm. Our children were the fatherless. God would be her defender. God would be a father to my children.

And there hasn't been a single moment of fear. Sadness? There's sadness. Loss? Sometimes I feel a great sense of loss . . . but no fear. Not one instant of fear.

I'm not looking for "Hezekiah years." When God told Hezekiah his life was over, the king turned his face to the wall and begged God to grant him more years. It was said of this king, "There was no one like him among all the kings of Judah, either before him or after him" (2 Kings 18:5). So God gave him fifteen more years. During those years Hezekiah showed his wealth to the Babylonians. When the prophet Isaiah told him that everything he had shown, as well as some of his sons, would be taken captive to Babylon, sadly, Hezekiah thought it was good. "There will be peace and security in my days," he said. A son he fathered in those years became king and "did more evil than the nations the LORD had destroyed before the Israelites" (2 Kings 21:9). It makes me wonder what would have happened if Hezekiah had accepted God's initial instructions to "put his house in order" rather than cry out for more years.

That's what we're trying to keep our eyes on here.

A few years ago, we asked God to teach us a new way to pray for this country because we weren't seeing any change. These were the words God gave us:

At any cost.
At any cost.
Shake this nation.
Break the strongholds.

That's the prayer God gave us to pray. I have prayed that prayer in the mosques and in my study and while walking the streets of Istanbul... day after day... year after year. God continually gave us chances to change that prayer.

We could have said,
Not at the cost of our children.
Not at the cost of a sixtieth wedding anniversary.

Not at the cost of having a home someday where we can write and go for long walks.

We could have replied to God's question with stipulations, but at each point He gave us the courage to say simply, *whatever the cost.*

Even now this is how I continue to pray: *God, I lay down my life, my hopes, my dreams, my reputation. I'm a sinful man with a checkered past. I wasn't always passionate for you, God. But I lay it all down. I lay this sickness down. Do whatever it takes to break the chains of bondage in Turkey. We are your servants.*

Pour us out.

Use us.

I tell everyone we have a marriage unlike any other.

CHAPTER 21
BY THE GRACE GOD HAS GIVEN

The jewels of a Christian are his afflictions. The regalia of the kings that God has made are their troubles, their sorrows, and their griefs. Griefs exalt us, and troubles lift us.

CHARLES SPURGEON

PERHAPS I MIGHT have lived a longer life if I had turned down this opportunity to die out loud, but it would have been a half-life. I don't believe that God will heal me. I would be thrilled if He did: I don't have a death wish. I'd like to see the kind of girl my son chooses for his wife. I'd like to watch my daughter play with her first child. I'd like to see my son stand on a platform and express his passion to reach Muslims for Christ.

But when I compare these desires with the fate of the lost people around me, the circle of people we've shared with you, this beautiful community of Muslim people, there's no choice. I'd much rather see them saved than see any of these shallow dreams come to fruition.

Our personal dreams can seem so big at times. Our visions of what the future should look like feel so important. We hold up our dreams as if they are gods, and we dedicate everything to bring them to pass—but in reality they are shallow dreams. Mud puddles. Real dreams involve seeing the lost saved. Real dreams involve seeing the spiritually dead live again.

Please don't think, "Oh, Stan and Ann are great people." We're not. We've lived our lives and made our decisions by the grace God has given us. Our courage has come directly from Him. The desire to face this honorably comes from God. There's not the smallest part of it that is our own. The willingness to do this comes from God and Him alone.

* * * * * *

Our Turkish friends said they are willing to help bury me, if that's what Ann and I would like. Would I mind being buried by my Muslim friends? Of course not! These are hands that love me, that care deeply for my family. Let them do whatever they need to do to process through their grief and to see that I am their brother, that I respect the love they have for us. I'm honored by all the ways they've blessed Ann, Elle, Stanley, and me.

They'll transport me hundreds of miles east, to the small village where I've received permission to be buried. We don't know of any other situation where a foreigner has been allowed to be buried along the Euphrates.

Our friends are looking for a house where Ann can live at the center of that village, across the street from the village elder, because they want to honor and protect her. These are the doors cancer has opened for us ... for Ann. They call her *Yenge* or "my brother's wife." It's an endearing term of respect, and it reflects just how deeply the community loves our family.

* * * * * *

I've been blessed with a nice study in our apartment, a room that's probably fifteen feet long and nine feet wide. There are two comfortable armchairs, a small ottoman, and a desk covered with pictures and mementos that are dear to me. There's a bookshelf with some of my favorite books: classic sermons and meditative literature. The floor is covered with various prayer rugs.

> "One of our family sayings is, 'No reserves, no retreats, no regrets.' When you're determined to live without regrets, your heart is in a better position to look for the good that comes from the bad. When you live without regrets, you live in the present and can see better where God is leading you today."
> —Stan

We bought one of the prayer rugs when it wasn't in great condition, and the tassels were terribly tangled. It took me hours to untie the knots, remove the twists, and straighten the threads. Once I'd done that I could comb through the tassels in a few seconds. As long as I comb them once in a while, there's little upkeep required.

It reminds me of my inner life and the way I'm confronted on a daily basis with this path before me. If I don't spend time keeping my spirit in line with God's plan, a lot of knots and tangles would

> *I keep my eyes always on the LORD.*
> *With him at my right hand, I will not be shaken.*
> *Therefore my heart is glad and my tongue rejoices;*
> *my body also will rest secure,*
> *because you will not abandon me to the realm of the dead,*
> *nor will you let your faithful one see decay.*
> *You make known to me the path of life;*
> *you will fill me with joy in your presence,*
> *with eternal pleasures at your right hand.*
>
> —Psalm 16:8-11

begin to form. But each and every day I allow God to comb through the tassels of my soul, and He keeps everything in line.

Stanley came into my study the other night while I was resting on the sofa. It's a low couch, without legs, so I was just about floor level. Outside it was already dark. If I listened carefully, I could hear the cars beeping their horns on the main street, a few roads over from where we live.

Then Elle and Ann came in. (Elle is taking online college courses from home for the time being.) This is how we've spent many of our evenings since the diagnosis, a quiet family of four. We try to keep a light tone most of the time, and we still laugh a lot, in spite of the circumstances. I was lying on the low sofa, and everyone else sat in their favorite spots in the room. Then Stanley said something that made my heart swell and my eyes brim.

"Well, my dad's going to be buried here, and I'm going to continue the work our family started together here. His body will be like a beachhead on the Euphrates, and I'm going forward from there."

✶ ✶ ✶ ✶ ✶ ✶

When we were in the States on furlough in 2009 my best friend here in Turkey Skyped me. He's on very good terms with the imam. We talked for a little while, and he told me what was going on in our Turkish community. He updated me on our Turkish family and how business was for our friend, the building contractor. He told me about the apartment building being built next to his shop. He complained about how his favorite soccer team was performing.

Then at the end of the call he told me something that gave me hope.

"The imam wants me to tell you that he's reading the Bible you gave him. He wants me to tell you that he's praying to Jesus, and that he now believes that Jesus is the greatest prophet."

For a Muslim to say that anyone besides Muhammad is the greatest prophet is unheard of. For him to put Christ over Muhammad . . . that's a big deal.

When I heard that news three years ago, I thought we were on the verge of something incredible. I thought we were turning the corner. But then we came back to Turkey and didn't see any fruit. The spiritual ground around us still looked barren. But this imam is reading the Word of God and praying to Jesus. And I'm still welcome to be with my Muslim friends and pray to Jesus. When people are seriously ill, they ask me to pray to Jesus for them.

While this is a shift in thinking, it's still not the groundswell of change that we've prayed for. The parched and barren lives around us desperately need the rivers of eternal life. So we continue to pray . . . and wait for the glass dome over Turkey to be shattered.

BY THE GRACE GOD HAS GIVEN

I can't wait to see how God will use my daughter, Elle.

CHAPTER 22

WHAT IS YOUR PART?

A general who served in India said to his son as he was dying, "Come see how a Christian can die."

SIR HENRY HAVELOCK (1795–1857)

IN THE FALL OF 2012, Elle delivered the following talk at a church in the United States:

I'm Elle Steward, and I'm a missionary kid from Turkey. Five weeks ago I left my parents, Stan and Ann, and my little brother, Stanley, in Istanbul and came here to attend a Christian college. In Turkey, I live among the people you call terrorists: anti-American, anti-Christian, Muslim.

I call them family.

From Istanbul to the border regions of Iran, Iraq, and Syria, to the Dark Canyon at the headwaters of the Euphrates, my family has been showered with love and kindness and hospitality. Three weeks ago my father was diagnosed with terminal cancer and now has months left to live. God has given my family unexplainable peace and confidence in His will.

But my Turkish family has been broken. They have no hope in death in their religion or culture and they have been shattered by this news. My parents have been hosting them constantly as my neighbors try to offer love and fruit juice and comfort. Village leaders, cell-phone shop owners, plumbers, and truck drivers have been calling my dad, offering anything they have, anything they can do to help.

People all across the country have been taking to their mosques to pray for us, and this past Friday the imam of the mosque in our Turkish community led his entire congregation in prayer for my father.

These are your terrorists?

These are your anti-American and anti-Christian embassy burners?

These are God's beloved, His chosen, His children . . . and my family. Jesus died and gave everything He had, down to His last drop of blood and gasp of air for these people. My dad is going to do the same, and so will I.

What part are you going to play in this? Are you going to send those who go? Are you going to pray for us?

Or are you going to take up the glorious task of bearing God's gospel to the unreached, unloved, and untouched people of Eurasia and give them a chance?

> Let nothing move you. Always give yourselves fully to the work of the Lord, because you know that your labor in the Lord is not in vain.
> —1 Corinthians 15:58

WHAT IS YOUR PART?

Planning and praying for our final expedition.

CHAPTER 23
DYING OUT LOUD

*They triumphed over him by the blood of the Lamb
and by the word of their testimony;
they did not love their lives so much
as to shrink from death.*

REVELATION 12:11

ANN CAME UP behind me the other day, put her arms around my neck, leaned her forehead on my shoulder, and started to cry.

"Oh, honey," she said quietly. "Oh, honey."

The emotion comes in waves like that.

During the entire course of our marriage, we've never fought. We've never been a sparring couple. There have never been any slammed doors or shouts. We've always done our best to encourage and uplift each other. Ours is such a special relationship.

If God would heal me, I'd be ecstatic. I want to live a long life with Ann. I want to live another thirty years with her. I want to walk the streets of Istanbul with her and see the smiles on the faces of our Turkish friends. I want to love on Muslim people and pray for them. And I want to do that with Ann.

But if it's God's plan to take me early, then that's what I want more than anything else. So each and every day I have to lay down my own desires, my own dreams, and my own expectations on how I always thought my life would look.

On that day when Ann came up behind me and I felt her love so strongly, I had to pray something that wasn't usually in my prayers.

God, I don't say this every day because I don't want to go down a road that will damage me, but today I lay down the dreams of what life was going to be like with Ann in the coming years, when it would have been just the two of us. It's hard to give that up.

This is the process of laying down our lives for God. It's not easy. It's not once and done. It's an ongoing process, a never-ending path . . . sometimes smooth, sometimes rocky. But if we can stay on that path, He will draw us ever closer to Himself.

* * * * * *

Some years ago we were out east, right on the border of northern Iraq, in a village where the government had forcibly evicted people to try and keep the terrorists from colluding. It was exactly the kind of place where God continually led us.

We sat around a fire having tea with a bunch of men. This was a dangerous place filled with dangerous men. It was hot outside and sweat trickled down the small of my back. Sweat dripped off of my face. I was uncomfortable and had drunk too much tea. As I scanned the faces of the men around the fire, I thought about all the chaos they were involved in, the havoc they were creating.

Here I am, I thought, *and this is the job God has given me.*

I almost started laughing. Never in my wildest dreams could I have come up with a scenario like that, yet it so closely matched the desire for adventure and danger I'd felt when I was growing up. Sitting there around that campfire, my soul filled with joy. I was on God's mission, full of purpose.

In that moment I remembered lying on my back in my grandfather's church when I was a boy. I remembered feeling the presence of God flowing with the wind through the windows and the sweet scent of summer. I remembered closing my eyes. I could hear again what God had said to me on that day, over forty years before.

I have a purpose for your life. I have a particular task that, if you do not do, will go undone.

I knew in that moment, hanging out with unsavory men around a fire in southeastern Turkey, that I was on the right road.

It's the same way that I feel today. It's the reason we can have joy even now. It's the reason I can die out loud.

> "You were created for a purpose. God has a plan that involves you, and if you don't complete the tasks He has for you, they may very well go undone. Seek Him with all your heart! Be open to the plan He has for you! While it may involve sacrifice, it will also fill the hole inside of you that cries out for meaning."
>
> —Stan

Today, as we work on this book, it's a Friday, and my Muslim neighbors are finishing up their main weekly service. My friends are there today praying for me, praying that God would heal me, praying that it would be God's will that I be healed. Others there pray for their sick children or that they would find work. They're praying for good spouses for their children. They're praying that their grandchildren grow up to be successful people, men and women of character.

> *One thing I ask from the LORD, this only do I seek: that I may dwell in the house of the LORD all the days of my life, to gaze on the beauty of the LORD and to seek him in his temple.*
>
> —Psalm 27:4

Yet they are totally hopeless and lost.

In our community, we are the only Christians that they can look at and say, they're doing it differently. They look at us and know in their hearts that we serve a different God. They know that I serve Jesus and God and the Holy Spirit, and when they see us confront life, they see a difference.

We need more people willing to live out their lives in front of Muslims. It's nothing more complex than that. You don't have to be a great linguist or preacher or theologian. You just have to be willing to come and live among Muslim people and show them the love of Christ ... show them how a Christian lives life. All you need to do is show them what kindness looks like, and joy, and faith, and hope.

There are over a billion Muslims in the world who've never heard the gospel. These are good people. They are worthy people. They deserve a chance to be saved. They deserve an opportunity to be saved, but in order for that to happen, they have to see a Christian life lived out. They have to see good days and bad days. They have to see life and death.

That's where we came up with the phrase, "Dying out loud." It would be a lot more comfortable for us to be at home right now with our families around us and doctors that speak English and good pain medicine. It would be comforting to know that hospice waited at the end to take care of things, to make my final hours more bearable.

But we have the opportunity to live our lives in front of Muslims and show them how a Christian lives and dies. No finger-pointing. No megaphones. Just us . . . living life. We've tried to show them how a Christian goes through good times and bad times. This is how we deal with a rent increase or a shortage of funds. This is how we approach sickness. This is how we respond when people unjustly accuse us. This is how a Christian navigates life.

You don't have to be a saint to live your life out in front of Muslim people. You just have to pray every day, *God, let me see them the way you see them.*

You just have to be willing to love them.

* * * * * *

One of my favorite pictures is of Stanley crossing a footbridge in central Turkey. The bridge crosses high over a wide river, perhaps 200 yards from one bank to the other. It's held together by cables about eight feet apart, and the planks are just placed on top of the cables. Some of the boards are rotten or missing, and if you look down through the gaps you can see a swollen river rushing fifty feet beneath the bridge.

The photo is taken from behind Stanley as he begins to cross this bridge. The cables along the sides are too far apart for him to reach, so there's nothing for him to hang on to. He walks carefully, his left foot reaching ahead tentatively, his arms out slightly for balance. Shrubs, boulders, and patches of grass line the far bank. It looks so far away. Off in the distance is a tree-covered mountain, then another beyond that, and another.

The bridge sways back and forth under Stanley's weight. He's only ten years old in that photo. But he's brave. And he's determined. He isn't looking at the far bank or the hills or the mountains. He's just looking at the space in front of him, deciding where to place his next step.

Sometimes this approach to death feels like crossing that bridge.

There's nothing for my hands to hold on to. I have to work hard to keep my balance because the bridge sways constantly beneath my feet. Below me, an infinite fall to a rushing river. Each step is so small, and the opposite bank, if I let myself look up, seems far away.

But even in the midst of this harrowing experience, I have to admit: I have a smile on my face. Because this is what I was created to do, and my Father is crossing with me. I can hear His voice encouraging me.

Death is just the next great adventure, and if there's even the smallest chance that my Muslim friends will come to Christ by watching me cross this bridge, then I will take each step willingly, for them. So I take another step . . . and then another. I can feel the breeze on my skin. I can hear the sound of water moving far beneath me. I feel myself gaining my balance and moving forward.

And I can hear my Father's voice, right there with me.

This is the purpose for which you were born. You can do it, Stan. You're almost there. I'm right here with you. I won't leave you.

So I take another step.

Stanley crossing the narrow footbridge.

*"I lift up my eyes to the mountains—
where does my help come from?
My help comes from the LORD,
the Maker of heaven and earth."*

— PSALM 121:1-2 —

Scan this code to watch a video
introduction to this chapter.

EPILOGUE

"WE'RE NEARING THE END," the doctor said, and Ann nodded a subtle, quiet nod, reaching up and holding Stan's hand. But he didn't respond. The machines went on and the IV dripped and Stan's eyes remained closed in pain.

"How long?" Ann asked.

"Anytime now. Perhaps up to 72 hours."

Dawn was breaking outside the hospital windows and the city sounded distant, muffled, like it was far, far away. The city Stan had loved, the city he would not walk through again.

"Thank you."

The doctor left the room, and Stan said in a barely audible voice, "It is almost over."

Ann started calling friends and family to let them know the end was near. Soon, there was a line of people waiting to see him. A chair was placed beside Stan's bed so each person could sit and have time to talk with him. These people were the friends and neighbors Stan had prayed for, ministered to, and befriended through their years living in Istanbul. Nurses peeked around the corner and asked each other who was so important that there was a line of people waiting to go into the room, a line of people waiting to see this man before he died.

"His name is Stan Steward." The word spread. "He is loved by so many Turks. Some say he is a holy man."

Friends sat in the chair and spoke quietly to Stan.

One man pulled out a strip of paper with Stan's handwriting on it. "Here is the scripture you sent to encourage me years ago. I've read it many times."

> "Wouldn't it be exciting if our last days were climactic with God, and not a quiet fading away? I want to go down swinging and fighting. I want to go out at the top of my game, not carried off the field in spiritual obscurity. I want to go out with dirt in my mouth, knuckles bruised and bleeding for my King."
>
> —Stan

Another man took out his phone and showed Stan a photo. "These are my children, the ones you prayed for when they were young. See how strong they are? See how tall they've grown? You prayed for them and they are doing well."

Sometimes Stan was awake, and he would nod or smile sleepily or whisper in English through the mountain of pain, and Ann would translate. He had lost the ability to speak Turkish in those final months. His friends would talk to him even while his eyes were closed and the machines beeped ever on. But the chair beside his bed remained occupied.

Members of the team arrived. Doug anointed Stan with oil, then sat in the corner praying continually.

Jesus.

Jesus.

Outside the hospital, throughout Istanbul, the people celebrated Ramadan, the ninth month of the Muslim year, when fasting is observed each day from the moment the sun comes up to the moment it goes down.

But on this night the city bustled as people prepared to break the fast; it was the night called *Kadır Gecesi*, or the Night of Power, one of the most sacred nights on the Islamic calendar. It celebrates when the Qur'an was revealed to the Prophet Muhammad. The Night of Power is also the night when God bestows blessings and sins can be forgiven, so people flock to their local mosques to recite the Qur'an and send blessings on the Prophet Muhammad. Some remain all night praying in the mosque.

The energy on the streets was palpable. The mosques were full of men bowing on their mats. Women worked in the kitchen, preparing the feast.

As evening approached, it would soon be time for Muslims to break the fast. Ann and her children began telling those visiting, "Go home, get some rest, prepare your meal."

"Thank you so much for coming," Ann said, looking around at the group. These were Stan's closest friends, those who didn't want to leave until he had passed. They were so faithful to Stan, even at the end. "Please, go home and be with your families. We'll let you know if anything happens."

Eventually, after the hallway had cleared, Stanley and Elle headed home to get ready for dinner, and the only ones left in the room were Stan, Ann, and her Muslim Turkish sister. Ann adjusted Stan's blankets. He was unconscious and seemed to finally be resting without pain. The trailing line of his heartbeat slowly moved across the monitor.

Ann and her sister sat together, marveling at everyone who had come to sit with Stan. He was now calm. He had been in such pain, the kind morphine couldn't even cut through, and to see him settle like that was both a relief to Ann and confirmation that the end was near.

"Did you see that?" Ann asked, breathless.

Her sister nodded.

"He's almost there. It's so good to see him relaxed." A sob caught in Ann's throat.

The hospital was quiet. The sun was dropping. The Night of Power had nearly arrived.

"You should go home, too," Ann suggested. "Your family needs you. Go, prepare the dinner to break your fast. I'll call if anything happens so you can go get the kids to bring them back."

They hugged and the woman left. The room was empty except for Stan and Ann. It seemed fitting. Ann thought back over all they had gone through together, back to when Stan had left the police force in San Diego, how they had traveled the U.S. raising support, their first years in Turkey and their treks to the Iranian borders and the Euphrates. Stan had always wanted to go farther, over that next hill. What an adventure life had been with him.

She looked down at this man who had been her partner in everything for so many years. One moment he was peacefully sleeping, and the next moment he was gone.

Stan died.

Ann leaned in. He wasn't breathing. She checked the machines. His heart had stopped. She laid her head on his chest once more—the end had come. She took a deep breath and stood, walking calmly across the room to the door, where she leaned into the hallway and beckoned over one of the doctors.

"It's over," she said. "He's at peace."

EPILOGUE

It was August 2, 2013.

"Stan passed," Ann told her Turkish sister over the phone. The phone was silent for a moment. "Can you get the kids?"

"When did he pass?" she asked.

"Just a minute ago. I was sitting right here with him."

"But what time, exactly?"

"He just passed," Ann emphasized, not sure what her Turkish sister was getting at. "I promised I would call you as soon as he died.

And so began the steady stream of people returning to say their goodbyes once more: neighborhood friends, Turks who had become family, leaders from the community, team members. They packed into the room and lined the hospital hallway.

When Doug arrived to pray, the room and hallway quieted. It was a precious moment where Stan's friends, Christian and Muslim, gathered together. When Doug finished, everyone began trickling back out of the hospital.

"What a beautiful time for your husband to pass," one of the nurses said to Ann.

"Thank you," Ann said. She knew it was an honor to die during Ramadan, so she thought that the nurse was referring to that. But nearly every Muslim person who walked out said the same thing to her.

"What a beautiful time for Stan to pass."

Ann had lived with the Turkish people for many years and knew they were hospitable in every way, so she nodded and smiled and thanked each of them. Once the room had nearly emptied, she worked with a few others to figure out what needed to happen with Stan's body. Soon, she was back outside, getting a ride home with her Turkish sister and brother.

As soon as they were in the car, her sister made the same comment, "What a beautiful time for Stan to pass."

Ann looked over at her. "What am I missing? Why is everyone saying it's a beautiful time for Stan to pass? Why do you keep asking me about the exact time?"

"It's the Night of Power."

"But that begins tomorrow."

"No, Ann, it began tonight, at sunset. At the call to prayer. The call to prayer was going on when you called me, that is why I asked you about the time. This is the holiest night of the year, the night when the heavens open and angels walk the earth, when miracles happen. During this Ramadan, the Night of Power has fallen on a Friday, our holy day!"

Ann sat quietly in the car as they wound their way through Istanbul. Tears gathered in her eyes. Her sister reached over and took her hand.

"What a holy man of God Stan was, and how much God must have loved him, to take him in that moment!"

Thankfully, because of Stan's methodical approach to his own approaching death, everything had been planned and scheduled ahead of time. His funeral was held at a small chapel run by Christian Armenians on consulate grounds inside the ancient walls of Constantinople. New Testaments that included a small family portrait signed by Stan were given out to everyone in attendance who wished to have one.

Early the next morning, Ann and a large contingent of friends and family boarded a plane for a two-hour flight out to the Euphrates. This was followed by a three and a half hour bus ride to

EPILOGUE

the village. The bus was arranged for by Stan's Muslim friends in the village, and a hearse carried Stan's body from the plane to the burial site.

While the group made their way to the bus, Ann and a few friends went to receive his body from the airlines and see to the transfer to the hearse. As they walked to his casket, one of their Turkish brothers came over to Ann.

"I will not leave Stan alone," he said quietly. "I will ride in the hearse and pray for him all the way to the village."

At first, the atmosphere in the bus was somber and subdued, everyone tired from the flight. Ann leaned her head back and closed her eyes, a mixture of emotions competing to take over. She had watched her husband suffer for months, so there was relief. The knowledge that his death was coming, and the fact that it was finished, filled her with peace. She had been grieving this loss for eleven months.

She was also exhausted, and thankful they had made all of these arrangements in the previous months and weeks. Grateful for all the friends who helped bring everything together. They had worked so hard to have the funeral and burial be culturally respectful without jeopardizing their Christian witness—burying him in a cloth? Sure. Celebrating his life ten days later? That was fine. Having an imam say Muslim prayers over him? No, that would risk their Christian witness.

It was time to keep going, keep caring for her kids, keep pointing her Muslim friends to Christ and the hope they had in Him. *Christ is my strength*, she repeated to herself.

There had been so many things to navigate. And now they were driving to the graveside, riding in a bus with all of Stan's closest friends and colleagues. She could tell her friends were struggling; Turks don't do well with death, not normally. They don't talk about it, and they wouldn't let Stan talk about it before he died.

But they do grieve very well, and before Ann knew it, people were taking turns telling funny stories about Stan. The whole bus would erupt in laughter, and then it would quiet, and she could hear people crying, and then someone else would tell a story. The miles passed this way, laughing and crying and remembering this man who had meant so much to each of them.

At one point, one of the team's leaders from the U.S. leaned over and asked Ann a question. "How do you see your future, Ann? Do you want to be a leader?"

"Oh, I'm not a leader," Ann insisted. "That's not a good fit for me. I'm a good supporter. I just don't do well with correcting others, which I think is important for a leader."

A crease appeared on his forehead and he contemplated what she had said. He nodded slowly. Then he leaned in and asked another question: "Could you be a mom?"

Ann's heart swelled. "I could do that."

She felt something shift in her. Could she be a mom to the people in Turkey, to young team members, and to the Turkish people they all loved so much?

Yes. Of course. She could do that.

The grave was dug, a hole in the ground. The hearse couldn't get close enough to the gravesite, so they transferred the coffin to an ambulance and drove it up the hillside. The group followed on foot, climbing the path above the river. The pallbearers gathered, with Stanley at the front right position. Stan's body was lowered down into Turkish soil.

EPILOGUE

Unless a grain of wheat is buried in the ground, dead to the world, it is never any more than a grain of wheat.

Ann looked around at the crowd gathered there on that day along the Euphrates. So many Turkish Muslim friends.

But if it is buried, it sprouts and reproduces itself many times over.

Stanley picked up the shovel and dropped the first scoop of dirt on Stan's grave. The sound of the dirt raining down on the coffin was tangible and harsh. Then the shovel was passed to all of Stan's friends. What an emotional time: young workers, shoveling dirt, weeping; their Turkish friends, shoveling dirt, wiping their eyes.

"Ann," one of the villagers said quietly, standing there with his wife.

But Ann was watching the grave fill with dirt.

"Ann," the villager said again, lifting up his hand and touching Ann on the shoulder. This immediately got Ann's attention because a man in the village would never touch a woman who was not his relative. She turned.

"Look," he said, pointing out over the Euphrates, and coming up out of the canyon was a flock of white doves. "Those birds do not come here. It's a sign from God, an angel, it is for Stan."

Many looked. Even those filling the grave paused, shielded their eyes against the sun, and watched the birds as they wheeled, graceful in the sky, then vanishing over the horizon.

At the moment Stan was buried, when the men stopped shoveling and people began drifting away from the gravesite, back down the hill, a realization hit Ann.

It is finished. Stan is buried. I cannot touch or talk to him again.

That was when it hit the hardest. Stan was gone. It was over.

She looked around. The gravesite handpicked by their friends in the village. In the distance, the Euphrates, and, beyond that, the villages Stan had wanted to go to next.

Stan was gone. But he couldn't have been buried in a more beautiful spot or in a place that would have meant more to him.

The next day, Ann's friends in the village showed her potential houses she could move into, and she noticed they were calling her a different name. They weren't calling her Ann Steward anymore. They were calling her a Turkish name—a name meaning "One with us."

Two months later, all the legal paperwork regarding Stan's death has been filed in the States, the kids are now settled into college, and Ann is walking through the Istanbul airport for the first time, returning to Turkey. The airport, the air, the people—everything is exactly as she remembers it.

The only difference is that Stan is not with her.

She approaches customs, wondering if they will let her through. The reason for their presence in Turkey had always been Stan's work as a travel writer. What would they say now when she tries to re-enter the country? Will they give her a hard time? Will they turn her away? She tries to stand up straight and look confident. She hands the customs official her passport.

He looks up at her, his face flat, emotionless.

"What is the purpose of your stay?"

Ann clears her throat nervously.

"My husband is buried here, and I'm here for him."

The man's face immediately softens. He stands up behind his desk. Something like compassion forms around his eyes, and he

EPILOGUE

gives her a kind smile.

"Please, come in, my sister," he says in Turkish. "It is so good to have you. Welcome back."

She smiles as tears well up in her eyes. Most Middle-Eastern countries believe that if you are buried in their soil, you are part of them.

Unless a grain of wheat is buried in the ground, dead to the world, it is never any more than a grain of wheat.

Ann, Elle, and Stanley stand in a gap along the Euphrates.

"I cry to you, LORD;
I say, 'You are my refuge,
my portion in the land of the living.'"
— PSALM 142:5 —

"Unmapped, unexplored by foreigners, unreached in every way . . . forgotten, until now."

—STAN

DYING OUT LOUD Journal

MIKE MURRAY

STAND IN THE GAP

I looked for someone among them who would build up the wall and stand before me in the gap on behalf of the land so I would not have to destroy it, but I found no one. Ezekiel 22:30

"Oh God, I stand in the gap today on behalf of Turks. God, raise up men and women who are so desperate to reach them that they feel as if they are going to die if they don't." —Stan's prayer journal

You've finished reading *Dying Out Loud*, and maybe you're wondering: *Now what?* The Steward family's story of obedience and sacrifice has captured your attention, and now you want to pray for Muslims. Or you might be hungry to spend time in the presence of Jesus, to hear His voice. Perhaps you sense that God is calling you to proclaim the good news in Turkey or elsewhere in the Muslim world.

Perhaps you've come to a point of total surrender to God's will: *Lord, I will go anywhere and do anything for You, no matter the cost.*

This journal provides a framework to help you pray for Turks and other unreached people groups in Turkey. It creates an environment to help you abide in Jesus, surrender to His will, hear His voice, and follow where He leads.

Stan's core message from the book will be our guide: "You were created for a purpose. God has a plan that involves you, and if you don't complete the tasks He has for you, they may very well go undone. Seek Him with all your heart! Be open to the plan He has for you! While it may involve sacrifice, it will also fill the hole inside of you that cries out for meaning" (page 225).

The twenty-eight daily readings are loosely organized into four weekly themes: abide, surrender, listen, and follow. Abiding in Christ—the Vine—is foundational to all else, and each theme builds on the previous one. As you progress through the journal, please pray each day for the land that Stan and Ann committed their lives to.

On the next page, you will find a resource to help you do this. "How to Pray for Turkey" is a list of twelve kingdom prayers that are especially relevant in the Muslim world. Please incorporate some or all of these prayers as you stand in the gap over the next twenty-eight days.

Welcome to the Dying Out Loud challenge.

HOW TO PRAY FOR TURKEY

Turkey is home to about 75 million people, and 99.5 percent of them are members of Muslim people groups. This means they have virtually no access to the gospel. Among the 53 million ethnic Turks in the country, only a few thousand are followers of Jesus. As you pray for Turkey and Turks, please remember the other unreached people groups as well, including Kurmanji Kurds (8 million), Turkish-speaking Kurds (5.8 million), Zaza-Dimlis (1.1 million), Lebanese Arabs (1.1 million), and Kabardians (1.1 million). For more information about the unreached peoples of Turkey, visit JoshuaProject.net.

Pray for laborers: Jesus told us to pray that the Lord would raise up laborers (diligent workers) for the harvest fields. Please pray that God would raise up missionaries from all over the world to plant the church together in Turkey (Matthew 9:37–38).

Pray for the conviction of sin: It is only through the knowledge of one's sinful state and subsequent repentance, which lead one to turn to Jesus, that a person is saved. Pray that the people of Turkey would feel and know the burden of sin and would come to Jesus for forgiveness and salvation (Matthew 11:28–30).

Pray for the cross to be unveiled: False religions and deceptive ideologies have blinded men and women from every group of people to the truths of the gospel. Please pray that God would unveil the cross and that the veil on the minds and spirits of the people of Turkey would be taken away (2 Corinthians 3:16–17).

Pray for faith and against fear: The Bible says that God has given His followers a spirit of power. Pray that believers among the Turks would be set free from a spirit of fear of what may come and would boldly proclaim the truth of the gospel (2 Timothy 1:6–8).

Pray for the Word of God to rise: God's Word is so much more powerful than anything we can say; it is a mighty lion that needs to be unleashed. Please pray for the Word of God (in written, oral, musical, and dramatic forms) to be translated and to rise among the unreached people groups of Turkey (Isaiah 55:10–11).

Pray that God will pour out His Spirit on all flesh: God has promised to pour out His Spirit on all flesh—men and women, young and old, rich and poor. Please pray that God would pour out His Spirit on the people of Turkey—that they would see dreams and visions of Jesus and would be powerfully saved and empowered to be His witnesses (Joel 2:28–32).

Pray that Jesus would unite the body of Christ: It is Jesus' desire that His followers be in one accord. Please pray that God would unite the body of Christ. Pray that Christians from around the world would work together to reach Turkey and that the people groups of Turkey would be joined to the body of Christ (John 17:20–23).

Pray for good soil: Pray that the hearts of the people of Turkey would be like good soil, ready to hear the gospel and respond (Mark 4:1–20).

Pray for peace: The Bible tells us to pray for the peace of Jerusalem (Psalm 122:6) and for the people among whom we live (1 Timothy 2:1–4). Pray that the people of Turkey would experience peace not only in their nation but also in their hearts. Pray for the peace that results when men and women are reconciled with God (John 14:27). Pray for women and men of peace (Luke 10:6) among the Turks and other unreached peoples of Turkey.

Pray for bold proclamation: Pray that believers in Turkey would proclaim the message of the gospel clearly, making the most of every opportunity God places before them (Colossians 4:2–5).

Pray against works-based salvation and legalism: Plead that the Turks will understand that hope for forgiveness and acceptance with God is available only through Jesus' work on the cross (1 Corinthians 1:18).

Pray for joy in persecution: Church history tells us that the church grows the most when persecution is present. Pray that the believers in Turkey will endure persecution in a Christlike manner and will give their lives for the sake of the gospel if necessary (1 Peter 2:21–23).

—Adapted from "Kingdom Prayers" in *Live Dead Joy*

"We expect signs and wonders.
We expect to be overcomers.
We expect darkness to flee."

—STAN

"Praying, true praying,
costs an outlay
of serious attention
and of time, which
flesh and blood
do not relish."

—E. M. BOUNDS

WEEK 1
Abide

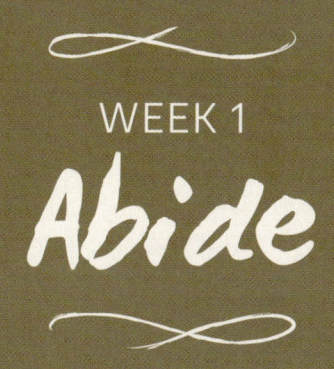

verb:
TO REMAIN IN PLACE;
TO CONTINUE TO BE SURE
OR FIRM, ENDURE.

DAY 1
ABIDE IN ME

"As the Father has loved me, so have I loved you. Now remain in my love." John 15:9

Jesus commands His followers to make disciples of all nations. In other words, He expects us to bear fruit to the ends of the earth. But in His goodness to us, our Lord doesn't merely issue an edict and walk away. He also reveals the secret to fruitfulness: abiding in Him.

In John 15:4–5 (NKJV), Jesus says: "Abide in Me, and I in you. As the branch cannot bear fruit of itself, unless it abides in the vine, neither can you, unless you abide in Me. I am the vine, you are the branches. He who abides in Me, and I in him, bears much fruit; for without Me you can do nothing."

Stan's priority each morning was to spend time with Jesus: worshiping, praying, studying Scripture, journaling, interceding for his neighbors. He viewed these hours as essential to fruitfulness in his local community. As he received life from the Vine, he was then able to share life with the lost around him.

WEEK ONE

Today, meditate on John 15:4–5. Ask the Holy Spirit to show you what it means to abide. In the space below, draw a picture of what abiding looks like, or write your thoughts on abiding. Make a commitment to abide in Jesus.

DAY 2
EACH AND EVERY DAY

One generation commends your works to another; they tell of your mighty acts. Psalm 145:4

Abiding in Jesus is a daily discipline. The psalmist wrote, "I will praise you every day" (Psalm 145:2, NLT), and Paul encourages believers to pray without ceasing (1 Thessalonians 5:17).

The Stewards dedicated one room of their Istanbul apartment to prayer and study. It featured maps of Turkey, photographs from their many expeditions across the country, and a generous supply of prayer books and devotionals. Stan and Ann purchased several prayer rugs for this room, and one such rug was in relatively poor condition. Stan spent hours repairing its tassels: untying knots, removing twists, straightening threads. Once this remedial work was finished, daily combing kept the tassels straight and free of tangles.

The process reminded Stan of his inner life: "If I didn't spend time keeping my spirit in line with God's plan, a lot of knots and tangles would begin to form. But each and every day, I allow God to comb through the tassels of my soul, and He keeps everything in line" (pages 213–14).

WEEK ONE

Today, ask the Father to give you a hunger to abide in Jesus every day. Commit to wake up earlier or to rearrange your schedule—whatever it takes to spend more time with Him. Write a prayer of commitment below.

DAY 3
MORNING DEW

∞

Who is wise? Let them realize these things. Who is discerning? Let them understand. The ways of the LORD are right; the righteous walk in them. . . . Hosea 14:9

"I will spend my mornings in prayer," Stan wrote in his prayer journal. "I will close out my day in prayer. When I hear the call to prayer, I will go into my room and pray for Turks."

Jesus began each day in prayer. David started his day by seeking and worshiping his Lord. Men and women of God through the centuries have followed the same pattern. In his prayer journal, Stan compared morning prayer to dew (Hosea 14:5; Psalm 133:3):

"When we lived in San Diego, we set our automatic sprinklers to water the lawn just before dawn. This was the optimal time for the lawn to absorb water. San Diego is a hot climate, and watering in the heat of the day can burn the grass, or the water could dissipate too quickly. But in the stillness of the morning, before the heat of the day, the water could be slowly and fully used by the grass."

WEEK ONE

Today, as you pray, ask for the refreshing, life-giving dew of the Holy Spirit. And as you continue through this journal, dedicate the first part of your day to abiding in Jesus. Write the steps you might take to ensure that you spend time in God's presence each morning.

DAY 4
ABIDING PRACTICES

I rise before dawn and cry for help; I have put my hope in your word. Psalm 119:147

In *The Live Dead Journal*, missionary and author Dick Brogden defines abiding as *"spending extravagant time with Jesus every day."* He encourages his readers to tithe their time to Jesus, to spend two and a half hours each day with Him. Such a deep commitment sounds intimidating—impossible, even—but we could say that variety is the spice of abiding.

Stan and Ann incorporated many spiritual disciplines into their abiding times; abiding is much more than presenting an endless list of requests to God. Some common abiding practices include Bible reading, worship, praying for the salvation of your family and friends (or even people you've never met), journaling, praying in the Spirit, meditating on and memorizing Scripture, listening for the voice of the Holy Spirit. Stan even changed his physical posture depending on his activity.

WEEK ONE

Today, as you pray, listen for the voice of the Spirit. Is Jesus asking for a tithe of your time? Ask the Spirit to show you which of these practices you should include in your abiding time and then record your thoughts below.

DAY 5
AT THE ALTAR

*"As for me and my household, we will serve the L*ORD.*" Joshua 24:15*

In the book, Stan recalled that he was just five years old when God first spoke to him. It happened at the altar of his grandfather's church, and the location of this event became extremely significant in Stan's life.

> The altar would come to represent ... a place to wait patiently for God, a place to seek His will. Throughout my life I've spent a lot of time praying at the altar in a variety of churches, and it's often been the place where God has spoken to me. (page 17)

When their children were still babies, Stan and Ann instituted a practice in their home they called family altar. Each night, they gathered, talked about the day, sang hymns, and prayed together—thanking God for prayers answered that day and asking Him for His presence and provision for the next.

WEEK ONE

Today, consider whether any physical location in your daily life would be appropriate for a personal "altar"—a place to meet daily with Jesus. As you pray, offer yourself as a living sacrifice to God (Romans 12). Meditate on what it means to be a living sacrifice and record your insights below.

Then, if possible, rearrange your physical surroundings as needed to accommodate an "altar."

DAY 6
MAKE ME USABLE

"Before praying, 'Lord, use me,' pray, 'Lord, make me usable.'" —Calvin Olson

A quick reading of Stan's journal reveals his greatest ambition in life. His prayer, his goal, his desire was to be used by God to reach the unreached—however and wherever his Master saw fit. He wrote:

> "Wouldn't it be exciting if our last days were climactic in our relationship with God, rather than a quiet fading away? I want to go down swinging and fighting. I want to go out at the top of my game and not be carried off the field to fade away in spiritual obscurity. I want to go out with dirt in my mouth, with my knuckles bleeding and bruised for the King."

Being used by God is thrilling, but it should also humble us that the Creator of the universe would find us usable and worthy of His attention. Being made usable can be a long and painful process, but it should be the goal of every servant of Jesus. As we abide in Him, He makes us more like Himself. As we abide in Him, He makes us usable.

WEEK ONE

Today, pray, "Lord, use me to fulfill Your purposes in the world. But first, do whatever it takes to make me usable." Ask the Holy Spirit to show you the areas in your life that must be refined in order for you to be a useful and usable instrument in the hands of Jesus. Record your thoughts below.

DAY 7
PRUNING

Since we are surrounded by such a great cloud of witnesses, let us throw off everything that hinders and the sin that so easily entangles. And let us run with perseverance the race marked out for us. Hebrews 12:1

The fig tree was growing rapidly, out of control, threatening to overwhelm a corner of the yard. Stan realized he had to do something, for the health of the tree and a future harvest of figs. So he cut it back to little more than a stump, hoping he hadn't killed it.

At the altar of his church the next night, Stan prayed a prayer that changed the course of his family's life: "God, I want more. I want You to prune me just like I pruned that fig tree yesterday. Just cut the extra stuff out of my life. Cut it out and let me focus on You and the plans You have for our family" (page 43).

God answered Stan's prayer. He removed the "extra stuff"—the career, the mortgage, the cultural expectations—so Stan and his family could pursue God's plan without distraction. Hebrews 12:1 encourages believers to "throw off everything that hinders." Sometimes, as God prunes us, He asks us to set aside what we might consider to be good things in order to fulfill His perfect plan.

WEEK ONE

Today, as you abide in Jesus, ask Him to prune you.
Ask Him to begin cutting away the extra, unnecessary parts
of your life—for your spiritual health and for the sake
of the spiritual fruit you might bear. Below, write about the
things—possessions, unhealthy relationships, sin, dreams,
ambitions—He is telling you must go.

"God, give me a spirit
and will that are totally
abandoned to you."

—STAN

WEEK 2
Surrender

verb:
TO YIELD (SOMETHING)
TO THE POSSESSION
OR POWER OF ANOTHER

DAY 8
I AM YOURS

Were the whole realm of nature mine,
That were a present far too small;
Love so amazing, so divine,
Demands my soul, my life, my all.
—"When I Survey the Wondrous Cross"
by Isaac Watts

The Steward family regularly sang hymns as part of their family altar time, and many of their favorites speak about giving all to Jesus. Stan's journal reveals that *surrender* was a recurring theme of his prayer life:

"Once again, I come to you today, Lord, and say that I am yours. My hopes, dreams, family, reputation, character, wants, desires—all are Yours to do with as You see best. I trust You. Give me peace and trust where I fail to possess them."

WEEK TWO

Today, as you abide in Jesus, ask Him to show you any areas of your life that you have not been willing to surrender. Are you having trouble trusting Him with your family? With your career? Ask Him for peace and trust in these areas, and write your insights below. As a reminder of your commitment to surrender all to Jesus, write "I Am Yours" on a piece of paper or a notecard and put it in a place where you will see it often.

DAY 9
A RIGID PATH

I consider everything a loss because of the surpassing worth of knowing Christ Jesus my Lord, for whose sake I have lost all things. Philippians 3:8

American consumer culture exerts constant pressure on followers of Jesus. Stan knew from experience that cultural expectations of living a "responsible" life can take us off the path God intended for us.

> We're bombarded with a multitude of messages: "Color inside the lines. Stay inside the box. Think responsibly. What are you going to be when you grow up? How are you going to make a living that will support a family?" Before you know it, you have a career, a mortgage, two car payments . . . and a rigid path set in front of you. (page 19)

In his journal, Stan said that a God-centered life is often found off of this path: "We are programmed to work hard so we can someday enjoy life and the good things that we have earned. But if you try to find a biblical model for this way of life, you will come up empty. . . . I believe that real living is found in abandonment to God and His purpose and not in our success, income, dreams, plans, hopes, or abilities."

WEEK TWO

Today, as you pray, ask the Holy Spirit to point out pressures and expectations of your culture that undermine your ability to pursue God's will. What are some things that your culture says are important—such as leisure, retirement, attaining and maintaining a certain lifestyle—but are of little or no value in the kingdom? Surrender these pressures to Jesus and write your insights below. If God is asking you to make changes in your lifestyle, take concrete steps to follow Him in obedience.

DAY 10
A SERVANT'S HEART

Serve one another humbly in love.
Galatians 5:13

Servanthood runs counter to our culture and human nature. If we're honest with ourselves, we'll admit that much of the time we would prefer to be served. In the kingdom, however, we are called to serve, to place others ahead of ourselves. We must surrender our desires. Jesus is our example. He said, "For even the Son of Man did not come to be served, but to serve, and to give his life as a ransom for many" (Mark 10:45).

In his prayer journal, Stan wrote, "I want to vigorously cultivate a servant's heart. My daily longing is to have my desires, wants, plans, hopes, and dreams torn out of my heart, and their void to be filled with the desires, wants, plans, hopes, and dreams of God. I want to die to self, to recognition, to status, to selfishness, to glory. I want to serve—not be served. Help me to keep this longing for genuine servanthood fresh and persistent each day."

WEEK TWO

Today, as you abide in Jesus, surrender your desire to be served and ask Him to give you a longing to lay down your life to serve others. Ask the Holy Spirit to show you practical ways to serve people in your life, and record your insights below.

DAY 11
TRUE ABANDONMENT

"The most important thing about any one of us is not what we do but what God does, not what we do for God but what God does for us." —Eugene Peterson

"True abandonment to God does not keep a tally of sacrifice or hardship," Stan wrote in his prayer journal. "True sacrifice does not consider itself a loss; rather, it is characterized by a longing and urgency for more of God. . . . I want the life that says, 'Nothing stands in the way or rivals my focus on fulfilling the purpose for which God has created me.'"

Stan understood that hardship and suffering would eventually equip him to fulfill that purpose. As the apostle Paul wrote: "We can rejoice, too, when we run into problems and trials, for we know that they help us develop endurance. And endurance develops strength of character, and character strengthens our confident hope of salvation" (Romans 5:3–5, NLT).

WEEK TWO

Today, in your abiding time, pray for the strength to live a life abandoned to God's purposes. Pray for the grace to rejoice when trials come. Thank the Lord that He doesn't waste our hardships but uses them to develop endurance, character, and hope. Meditate on these verses in Romans and write about the truths the Spirit speaks to you.

DAY 12
LIKE A CANDLE

"My Father, if it is possible, may this cup be taken from me. Yet not as I will, but as you will."
Matthew 26:39

Paul wrote in 1 Corinthians 15:31 (NKJV), "I die daily." John the Baptizer said of Jesus, "He must become greater and greater, and I must become less and less" (John 3:30, NLT). This daily dying to self means that the will and plan of Jesus continually grow in our hearts and minds while our dreams and desires dissolve to nothing. As we make a practice of abiding in Jesus, eventually His desires and passions become our own.

In his journal, Stan compared this abandoned, crucified life with a candle. He prayed, "Give me the strength to live as a wick that gives light only as it dies."

WEEK TWO

Today, as you pray, light a candle and watch the wick shrink as it burns. Meditate on what it means to die to self. How can dying to self—surrendering our hopes, dreams, and agendas—give light to those around us? Write or draw your thoughts below.

DAY 13
ALL WILL SUFFER

It has been granted to you on behalf of Christ not only to believe in him, but also to suffer for him.
Philippians 1:29

"The question that God asked Ann is such an important one for this generation: 'Are you willing to suffer?' The truth is, all of us will suffer, whether or not we're willing. If we approach suffering with an unwilling heart, if we fight against it and seek to avoid it at all cost, it can destroy us. But if we're willing to suffer, if we're open to what God can accomplish through our suffering, then our joy and hope will be evident to everyone around us" (page 179).

Stan understood that even this willingness to suffer comes as a gift from God. It's not something we attain on our own. In his journal, he wrote, "I have always thought I could suffer for Christ, as long as I could choose the 'suffering.' Giving my family to God to 'do as He sees best' for them is a standard of my daily prayer life. It also, sometimes, scares me."

WEEK TWO

Today, as you abide in Jesus, examine your heart. Invite the Holy Spirit to show you whether you have been unwilling to suffer for Him. What scares you most about possible suffering? The One who suffered unjustly on our behalf will give us the grace to endure—and the joy to bring glory to Him. What would suffering for Jesus look like in your life? Surrender to Him your ideas of comfort and security, and process your thoughts in the space below.

DAY 14
COUNT THE COST

"I consider my life worth nothing to me; my only aim is to finish the race and complete the task the Lord Jesus has given me—the task of testifying to the good news of God's grace." Acts 20:24

"Anything worth something has a cost," Stan said in *Dying Out Loud*. In the same way that precious things cannot be bought without large sums of money, important transitions cannot happen unless someone pays the price.

Luke 14:28 says, "Suppose one of you wants to build a tower. Won't you first sit down and estimate the cost to see if you have enough money to complete it?" What would you like to see happen in the lives of those around you? Have you counted the cost? (page 188).

In his journal, Stan contemplated the cost of being light in a dark place, of treasuring Jesus in the midst of their community: "To pray at the heart of the enemy's camp, to praise the name of Jesus at the altar of Islam, is an honor that few Christians have had—not because it's rare, but because it is often too hard to invest the time and love to find favor in the community. . . . It is not an area where a few short years will pay off in big dividends. We believe it takes a commitment to dig in one spot long enough to hit bottom."

WEEK TWO

Today, in the space below, answer Stan's question: What would you like to see God do in the people in your life? List three to five people, and write a prayer for each of them. As you pray, contemplate what it will cost you to see this happen. Will it cost you hours, as you pray more often for them or spend more time with them? Will it cost you your reputation, as you proclaim the Word of God? Will it cost you comfort, as you attempt something new for the kingdom?

"To know the will of God,
we need an open Bible
and an open map."

—WILLIAM CAREY

WEEK 3
Listen

verb:

MAKE AN EFFORT
TO HEAR SOMETHING;
BE ALERT AND READY
TO HEAR SOMETHING

DAY 15
OPEN HANDS

"Our ultimate joy comes only from following Christ all the way to heaven." —Dale Ahlquist

When we have committed to a lifestyle of abiding in Jesus and have surrendered our plans, dreams, and agendas to His will, we are finally in a spiritual environment that is conducive to hearing His voice.

In his journal, Stan wrote, "I want to worship God with abandonment . . . to abandon everything that stands in the way of being worshipfully obedient to His plan and purpose for me and my family. . . . God, give me a spirit and will that are totally abandoned to You."

Living with true abandonment is more than a one-time event; it's a daily decision. Some followers of Jesus find it helpful to incorporate specific physical postures in their daily prayers to emphasize surrender and submission, such as kneeling or lying facedown on the floor.

Another practice is to pray with open hands, offering to God both the things He has given us (health, family, vocation) and the things He has not given us (fear, condemnation, doubt). After emptying our hands, we are free to receive what He wants to give us for that day.

Today, in your abiding time, practice the prayer of open hands. Show Jesus that you hold tightly to nothing but Him. Then quietly receive from Him. What is He speaking to you? Where is He leading? Record your thoughts below.

DAY 16
WE ASKED GOD

"I am the Lord your God, who teaches you what is best for you, who directs you in the way you should go."
Isaiah 48:17

One of Stan's favorite quotations comes from David Livingstone, the well-known medical missionary to Africa in the nineteenth century. "I am ready to go anywhere," Livingstone said, "provided it be forward."

For Stan, shortly after arriving in Turkey, "forward" meant east—to the border regions near Iran, Iraq, and Syria, areas populated by shepherds, nomads, and warlords. "I thought we should go," Stan said, "so we asked God about it."

After praying about the possibility, the Stewards sensed the Lord was giving them a green light. "We came to a conclusion: We wouldn't know exactly what it would look like, but we knew it was where God was leading us. We made plans to head east" (page 95).

WEEK THREE

Today, in your abiding time, think about the decisions you face right now, both large and small. Have you asked God about them? In the space below, list two or three circumstances in which you need direction, and write what the Holy Spirit speaks to you.

DAY 17
DISCOVER THE TRACK

*Whether you turn to the right or to the left,
your ears will hear a voice behind you, saying,
"This is the way; walk in it." Isaiah 30:21*

Whenever the Stewards prepared for one of their Silk Road expeditions into central and eastern Turkey, they committed the entire process to prayer. They wanted nothing less than to be led by the Spirit on every trail they followed and in every village they visited. And after receiving direction from God, they moved ahead with purpose.

In a newsletter just before an expedition in 2012, Stan wrote, "We will be attempting to reach the most remote villages in the whole of Anatolia. We are told by the locals that most of these places have never been seen by Westerners. The possibility that we are the first believers to walk in these dark places demands our greatest diligence.... We expect signs and wonders. We expect to be overcomers. We expect darkness to flee."

In this way, the Steward family followed the pattern of the first missionary in this region of the world. F. B. Meyer wrote: "The apostle Paul did not have to cut or carve his way but simply had to discover the track that God had prepared for his steps from of old. And when he found it, it . . . would be the very pathway for which his character and gifts were most adapted" (page 93).

WEEK THREE

Today, as you abide in Jesus, write about a time in your life when you knew you were on the track that God had prepared for you. What were the circumstances that led you to that place? How did you make those decisions? Can you see that God was directing you, even when life was difficult? If you cannot recall such a time, pray that God would help you to hear His plan for your steps going forward.

DAY 18
KEYS TO HEARING

"Call to me and I will answer you, and will tell you great and hidden things that you have not known."
Jeremiah 33:3 (ESV)

As we ask God for guidance and direction, there are a number of practices that will declutter our lives and block out the "noise" so we can hear His voice. Three short prayers in Stan's journal give us a good place to start:

Lord, help me to understand this: "Be silent." First, turn off the TV, close your laptop, and walk away from your phone. Finding a place of solitude and stillness away from the urgent yet unimportant demands of daily life will show God that time with Him is your priority.

Help me to find full blessing and contentment in living for You. Next, watch your motives. God is not a vending machine that exists to give us what we want when we slide our coins into the slot. We must not view our abiding time as a transaction—even in those moments when we are seeking a specific word of direction. He is the reward.

Give me a heart that is open to Your lessons and discipline. Finally, adopt an attitude of humility. A teachable attitude will allow you to hear what God is saying through the Holy Spirit, Scripture, and other people. Consider what He might be teaching you in every circumstance you face.

WEEK THREE

Today, as you pray, examine your motives for abiding in Christ. Are you pursuing Jesus, or are you seeking what He can give you? In the space below, write about Scriptures you have read recently or conversations you have had that God is using to speak to you.

DAY 19
MANY ADVISERS

There is safety in having many advisers.
Proverbs 11:14 (NLT)

A few months after he was diagnosed with terminal cancer, Stan addressed a roomful of friends and colleagues in Istanbul—fellow missionaries serving in Turkey. The talk was typical Stan: passionate, funny, direct. He reflected on his illness, told some stories from his journey, and shared advice on several topics, including mentors.

Stan talked about some of his mentors through the years, such as those mentioned in *Dying Out Loud*: Calvin and Marian Olson, Abdullah, Marc. And he encouraged everyone in the room, no matter how experienced, to find at least one mentor. He even said that one of his mentors—a highly educated and widely published man in his late seventies who has worked in the Muslim world for decades—has a mentor of his own.

Stan's advice is biblical, of course, and is relevant to all of God's people, not just missionaries.

WEEK THREE

Today, as you abide in Jesus, ask Him to give you mentors, people who will challenge you to grow and will walk alongside you on your journey toward becoming like Christ. Rather than strategizing and thinking analytically, pray, "I trust You, Lord, to lead me to the right mentors." He knows what you need more than you do. As you sense the Holy Spirit giving you names, write them in the space below. Pray for wisdom about how to proceed.

DAY 20
LEARNING TO WAIT

"We can count on God to lead us into whatever we are to do." —Dallas Willard

The men in Stan and Ann's neighborhood prayed at the local mosque every Friday at midday. As Stan built friendships with these men, some of them invited him to their weekly prayers. Not yet an expert in the culture or Islamic tradition, he was confronted by his own questions: *Could I go to the mosque and pray to Jesus? What kind of message would this send to our community? Would I be welcome there, or would my presence cause unnecessary offense?*

Stan prayed about his options—and he also called four of his mentors to ask them about his situation. Two said, "Absolutely, go for it." The other two said, "Absolutely not. Don't do it." Because their decision was split, Stan prayed and waited. "I'm not going to force this to happen," he prayed. "I want it to be anointed. I don't want to make a mistake with this."

We don't like to wait. Our culture preaches instant gratification, and our consumer infrastructure delivers: fast food, movies on demand, vacation by credit card. This cultural impatience infects our spiritual life, especially when we want guidance or an answer to prayer. Patience is a fruit of the Spirit, a gift available for the asking. In God's *good* time, He will answer. Sometimes God tells us no. The "no" of the Spirit is just as important as His "yes." We must be obedient to both.

WEEK THREE

Today, as you abide in Jesus, ask Him to teach you patience. Ask Him for the wisdom to recognize His timing is best. Ask Him for the endurance to wait for the answer. In the space below, write about a time when it seemed God was slow in responding to your request. Can you now see that His timing was perfect?

DAY 21
WHAT HE WANTS

∞

"I have been crucified with Christ and I no longer live, but Christ lives in me." Galatians 2:20

"When I was growing up," Stan said in *Dying Out Loud*, "the Apollo program was in full swing, and teachers everywhere told children they could be anything they wanted to be. But God impressed on my life that I couldn't become anything I wanted to be—I could become what He wanted me to be" (page 21).

We have reached the end of Week 3 in our journal, a week dedicated to thoughts about guidance, direction, and hearing the voice of God. This is a scary topic for some. The reality is that many people are content not to hear. They suffer from a "Jonah complex": They are afraid that God will tell them to do something uncomfortable or sacrificial or dangerous.

If this is your fear, it will be helpful to keep in mind one simple fact: Our heavenly Father is good. As Mark Renfroe writes in *Live Dead the Journey*, "Luke 11 directly links the goodness of the Father to the work of the Holy Spirit. The Holy Spirit only guides us to those places where our loving and good heavenly Father is waiting for us."

WEEK THREE

Today, during your abiding time, use the space below to process your thoughts about who God wants you to be or what He wants you to do. Are you afraid that God will call you to do something you don't want to do? Has this fear kept you from seeking intimacy with Him? Ask Him to remove this fear and to remind you of His goodness.

"God isn't looking for people of great faith, but for individuals ready to follow Him."

—HUDSON TAYLOR

WEEK 4
Follow

verb:

STRIVE AFTER; AIM AT

DAY 22

THERE IS MORE

His master replied, "Well done, good and faithful servant!"
Matthew 25:21

There is more. This idea was a recurring theme in Stan's life. He wrote the following paragraphs, found in his prayer journal, at least a decade before his death:

"The heroes of the Bible allowed God to take them out of the status quo. They lived lives that we consider legendary because of their sacrifice, determination, and intensity. But they did something even more amazing—they went further with God.

"A prophet who lost all because of his obedience, a king who repeatedly humbled himself before God, a young Jewish girl who stepped into history by her willingness to lay it all on the line to save her people—these men and women said, 'I want something more.' They did not seek houses, transportation, promotions, plaudits, and power. These legends wanted to be completely used up for the purpose and opportunity of being a tool for God.

"Something inside of them dug deep into the will of God and said, 'This is what I live for.' I can't recall a single one of these who retired and lived a peaceful, enjoyable life. These revolutionaries worked until they dropped, died of illness, or were killed. There are no stories of a grand retirement, because the focus was on God's purpose, not their reward. They didn't have a quiet ending. The trials, troubles, and testing increased as they closed out their days on earth. They grew in power spiritually, they grew in influence and controversy, they grew in effectiveness, until they left this earth in death.

"This is what I want. My heart cries out and longs to be focused only on what God has for me. I want to finish well."

Today, as you abide in Jesus, meditate on the idea of "something more." Can you say of God's will, "This is what I live for?" Where is He leading you, both physically and spiritually? Write a prayer that commits you to going deeper with Him.

DAY 23

DEEPER INTO THE WORLD

"The spiritual life does not remove us from the world but leads us deeper into it." —Henri Nouwen

The month before Stan was diagnosed with terminal cancer, he was in remote eastern Turkey, with Ann and Stanley, on one of the family's frequent Silk Road expeditions. As he was able, Stan posted updates to his Facebook account. He wrote this dispatch on August 19, 2012:

"Back to our Euphrates base tonight after a wonderful day of steep roads, dust, steppe, and shepherds. We made it to the end of the road . . . only to find more goat trails to follow. Unmapped, unexplored by foreigners, unreached in every way . . . forgotten, until now. We explored the goat trails until we began to lose the sun. Six new families to add to our circuit, four of them nomadic shepherd clans. Promised to return. . . . Drank lots of warm goat milk mixed with baking soda to seal our new friendship. Overwhelmed at the possibilities."

A lifestyle of abiding gives both the motivation and the ability to move deeper into the world. Stan understood this. As we abide in Jesus, we come to love Him more. As we love Him more, He gives us the passion to share Him with others. And as we step out—sometimes on forgotten goat trails along the ancient Silk Road, sometimes on our school campuses in the suburbs—the Spirit works through us to draw people to Jesus.

Today, in your abiding time, pray for guidance and courage to move deeper into the world. Where, specifically, is God asking you to begin? Ask Him for more of the Holy Spirit, for both the passion and ability to make disciples. Write what you hear the Spirit say to you.

DAY 24
WILLING TO LOVE THEM

"To bless, to save, to help another, will fill our hearts with the most unalloyed blessedness of which the heart is capable." —F. B. Meyer

"You don't have to be a saint to live your life out in front of Muslim people," Stan said in the book. "You just have to pray every day, *God, let me see them the way You see them.* You just have to be willing to love them" (page 227).

So how does this work in real life? An excerpt from Stan's journal reveals how love can change perceptions:

"We were first viewed as a novelty: 'This is my American friend.' Then, once we had demonstrated longevity and staying power in the community, we were targets for conversion to Islam. Eventually, we were viewed as good people by some, a mystery to others, and a problem to a few. The weight of the imam's affection for us, along with the mosque elders, has bought us favor from those on the sidelines.

"Currently, there are only a few people we feel would rather not have us around—and even on them God has been working. The most fanatical of those few had a son serving in a hot zone for terrorism. We've traveled in that area and are well known there. During the course of his son's assignment, I would check in several times a week as to his safety. I called from the States to inquire when I heard of the deaths of soldiers. I counted the days until his discharge, and on August 10, he came home safe. The next time I was at prayer, the father came and ... put his arm around me and hugged me. Perseverance, perseverance, perseverance."

Today, as you pray, consider where God is leading you into deeper community with the lost around you. Is He giving you specific names? What might your involvement look like? What will it cost? Write your thoughts below.

DAY 25
THE DARK CANYON

"The thief comes only to steal and kill and destroy; I have come that they may have life, and have it to the full." John 10:10

In Stan's final months, his thoughts were never far from the unreached peoples of Turkey—the ethnolinguistic groups that have little or no access to the gospel, the people groups that will never hear the good news unless we go to them. Here is one of Stan's Facebook posts from October 2012:

> In bed, in the dark for the past three hours, thinking over the last six weeks: From the best Silk Road expedition ever to eight months to live, give or take. Terminal cancer. And yet, I can't escape the passion and vision we have carried this last year to buy a village house in the Dark Canyon of the Euphrates and open a house of light and prayer, a place of pilgrimage for teams who want to intercede for the unreached. . . . Crazy dreams of an (apparently) dying man. Maybe not. . . . I believe with all my heart we can still do this . . . even more so now than before.

In *Dying Out Loud*, Stan said of this area: "This

WEEK FOUR

Dark Canyon used to be an ancient shortcut, a part of Turkey where the original Silk Road passed by. The road has been there for a thousand years and passes through village after village after village.... Very few of the people in those villages have ever heard of the gospel. They all need someone to come alongside them, to share the good news with them. But it's not going to be reached in a week or two, or even a year or two" (page 130).

Today, as you abide in Jesus, intercede for the villages of the Dark Canyon of the Euphrates. Pray that followers of Jesus will go there to proclaim the good news, that the gospel will take root in the hard terrain, that churches will spring up and reach the entire region. In the space below, write a prayer for the people of the Dark Canyon.

DAY 26
STAN'S PRAYER

"Prayer doesn't just change circumstances; more important, it changes us." —Mark Batterson

"Looking out over a dark and sleeping city of 17 million, I realize again how blessed I am to live among so many who are lost," Stan posted on Facebook in November 2012. "When I add the villages of the Euphrates to the equation, it makes me weep with hope. . . . My soul sings this morning in Istanbul. I love my purpose."

God called the Steward family to treasure Him among the Muslims of Istanbul. As they loved Him, they grew to love the city of their calling. But how can anyone reach a city with millions of people? Stan, Ann, Elle, and Stanley began by loving and praying for their neighbors: the shopkeeper who sold them their phones, the vegetable sellers in the *pazar*, the guys from the neighborhood mosque.

This is how Stan prayed for his friends:

"Dear God, in all the men around me, break down the walls of their hearts right now. Open their eyes, God. Break down the wall of Islam. Demolish this stronghold. Let fountains of truth erupt out of the floor they kneel on. Let fountains of truth flow so that these people will see You and hear You and know You. Immediately, right now, imprint on their hearts and minds the name of Jesus. While they're praying, visit them supernaturally. Stamp the name of Jesus the Savior on their souls. We claim this territory by Your blood, and we drive back the forces of Satan. We drive back the darkness. We destroy the strongholds of Satan in the name of Jesus Christ." (pages 133–34)

Today, as you abide in Jesus, echo Stan's prayer for his mosque community. Pray for the men who will visit that mosque this week. You don't know their names, but the Father does. In the space below, rewrite this prayer on behalf of every mosque across Turkey.

DAY 27
SOW WITH TEARS

Those who sow in tears shall reap with shouts of joy. He who goes out weeping, bearing the seed for sowing, shall come home with shouts of joy, bringing his sheaves with him. Psalm 126:5–6 (ESV)

Spiritual harvest requires both seed and tears. When the Stewards were sent out as missionaries, the speaker at their commissioning service addressed this reality of the harvest: "[He] said that if we wanted to reap a harvest," Stan said, "we would have to moisten the dry ground with tears over the lost."

When Stan, Ann, Elle, and Stanley arrived in Turkey, they found soil that had been dried out for centuries. Carrying with them the seed of the gospel, they set about moistening the hard, dry ground. As their circle of friends and acquaintances grew, both in Istanbul and in the Euphrates region, they literally wept for the lost. Daily, they shed tears for their neighbors, looking ahead to a joyful harvest.

Stan's ministry of tears continued to his final days. Just weeks before he died, he wrote on Facebook about a friend he loved dearly: "The General showed up to visit me and harry the [hospital] staff to make sure all was being done to meet my needs.... Please pray for the General to meet Jesus and live his remaining days for Christ. He sat on my bed holding my hand and repeatedly kissed it. Oh, God, do not let him be lost!"

WEEK FOUR

Today, as you abide in Jesus, meditate on Psalm 126:5–6. Ask God to break your heart for the lost, to give you His heart for those far from Him. Begin praying for the people in your life who are lost without Jesus and write a prayer for them below.

DAY 28
ARE YOU CALLED?

He said to them, "Go into all the world and preach the gospel to all creation." Mark 16:15

Abdullah's finger jabbed at Stan's chest, while the words jabbed at Stan's heart: "Are you called? . . . Who are you called to?" (page 39).

God is calling you to someone. He is calling you to pray, to give, to go.

In February 2013, on his Facebook page, Stan quoted author Andrew Murray: "But how much greater the glory of intercession—when a man makes bold to say to God what he desires for others and seeks to bring down on one soul, or it may be on hundreds and thousands, the power of the eternal with all its blessings."

Will you follow Jesus deeper into prayer? Will you seek to bring down the power of the eternal?

In his prayer journal, Stan wrote: "God, challenge us to give freely, sacrificially, without any piousness of spirit. Thank You for giving us a heart to give back to You. You have blessed us so much! You have proved Yourself over and over throughout the years. 'Where your treasure is, there your heart will be also.'" Will you follow Jesus deeper into sacrificial giving? Will you invest your treasure in the mission of making Jesus famous among those who have never heard of Him?

Will you go? "These relationships are the only link to a physical representative of Christ that most of these families have ever had," Stan wrote in his journal. "There is intense oppression from Satan; we are drained physically, spiritually, and mentally after Friday prayers. But the opportunity to love on Muslims from the inside of the culture is a unique thing."

Will you follow Jesus to the ends of the earth? Will you give up your comfort and security to love Muslims in their communities?

> Today, as you abide in Jesus, answer these questions: Am I called? To whom am I called? Am I willing to intercede for the lost and for those trying to reach them? Am I willing to give sacrificially so the unreached can hear the gospel? Am I willing to follow Jesus wherever He leads?

ABOUT THE AUTHORS

Shawn Smucker is an author, blogger, and speaker who is passionate about story-telling and the importance of living an adventurous life. His book *Building a Life Out of Words* is consistently listed in Amazon's Top-Rated Memoirs/Biographies, and his most recent book, *How to Use a Runaway Truck Ramp*, details the 10,000-mile cross-country journey his family of six embarked on in a big blue bus previously owned by Willie Nelson. He is a regular contributor at Deeper Church, Prodigal Magazine, ChurchLeaders.com, and numerous other blogs and online publications.

Shawn received his English degree from Messiah College and currently lives in Lancaster, Pennsylvania, with his wife and four children. You can find him on Twitter, Facebook, and at shawnsmucker.com.

Michael Murray was an award-winning journalist before moving to Central Eurasia to serve in university ministry and church planting. His books include *Surrender All*, a one-year daily devotional, and *Grace & Truth*, a 90-day devotional journey through the Gospels. He and his wife, Nikki, have three children: Anna, Evan, and Colin.

Visit www.DyingOutLoudChallenge.org for more information about joining the Dying Out Loud community, taking a prayer trip to Turkey, or serving as a missionary in Turkey or elsewhere in Eurasia.

Also available from

LIVE | DEAD

The Live Dead Journal

Live Dead The Journey

Live Dead The Story

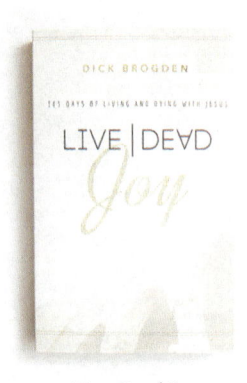

Live Dead Joy

The Live Dead Journal:
Her Heart Speaks

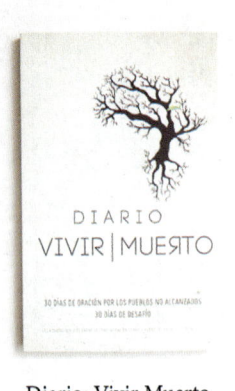

Diario: Vivir Muerto

Live Dead Life

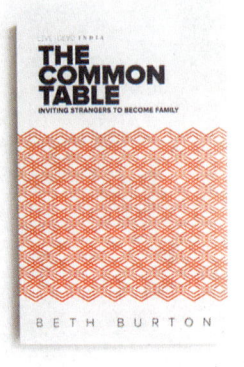

Live Dead India:
The Common Table

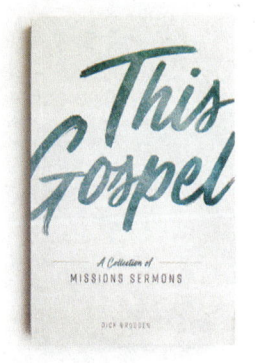

This Gospel

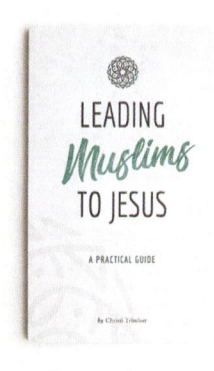

Leading Muslims to Jesus

Live Dead Together

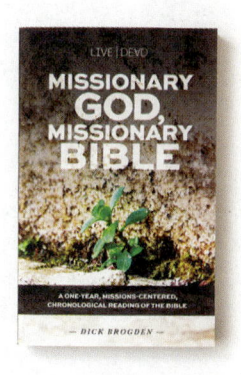

Missionary God, Missionary Bible

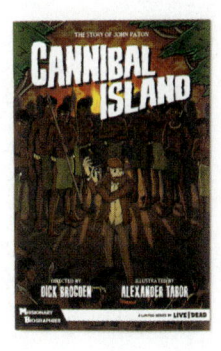

Cannibal Island

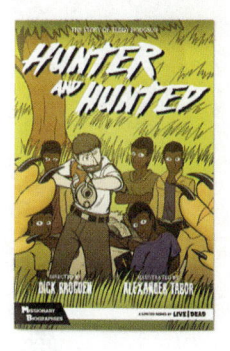

Hunter and Hunted

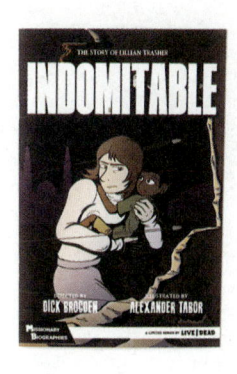

Indomitable

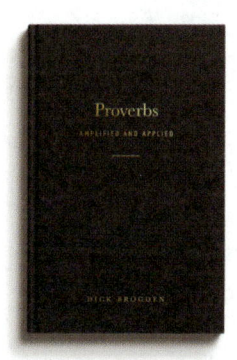

Proverbs

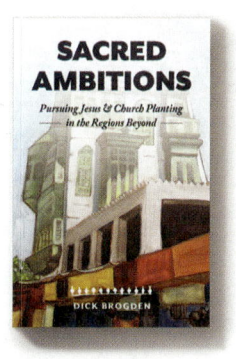

Sacred Ambitions

Check out our full line of Live Dead books at
www.abidepublishers.com which include:

Individual and group devotionals
Graphic novel biographies of missionaries
Challenging and inspiring stories from work among unreached people